OCEANS
OF
MY MIND

SCOTT STILLMAN

OCEANS OF MY MIND

WILD
SOUL
PRESS

Wild Soul Press
Boulder, Colorado

Editor: Emma Mure
Copy Editor: Sam Wright

Library of Congress Cataloging-in-Publication Data
Stillman, Scott
Oceans Of My Mind / Scott Stillman

LCCN 2022914909

ISBN: 978-1-7323522-8-5

For Valerie.

Contents

"The sea is a desert of waves, a wilderness of water."

—Langston Hughes

Preface

This is not a book about the fate of our oceans. Or the merciless slaughter of dolphins. Or the dying sea turtles and plastic bottles and acidification of seawater. If you want to read about these matters, try Rachael Carson's *The Sea Around Us*, Sylvia Earle's *The World Is Blue*, Cynthia Barnett's *The Sound Of The Sea*. There are others... written by environmentalists more credible than myself. I'm no marine biologist. I just know that whatever happens to the sea happens to ourselves. Our fates are intertwined.

But you know these things. Yes? Yes? Am I not speaking to the choir? Would another such book save the seas? Save the planet? Save the human race? I'd like to think so. But again, this is not that kind of book.

Occasionally we need a break from the gloom and doom of the world. Sometimes what we need is hope. A reason to get out of bed in the morning. A reason to live another day.

We must have escapes. Emergency exits. Portals to secret worlds where we can sneak away for a while—reclaim our souls. Without escapes, we'd surely go insane. It could be a forest meadow, a neighborhood park, a secluded beach. Or perhaps it's the pub, the coffee shop, the library, the casino. Or a sailboat in the wind, a fish on the line, a surfboard on a breaking wave. The *back of beyond...* whatever that means. A break from life, from whatever reality you've found yourself trapped in at the moment.

I've had many escapes. They fill the pages of my books—lonely desert canyons, lofty mountain ranges, dusty old roads to who-knows-where. Away from people, pollution, progress. Places where I can hear myself think, put things into perspective, regain my sanity.

Solitude can be a powerful healer, but it's not always the right medicine. Sometimes we need to experience some semblance of normalcy. Smiling faces, easy conversation—*connection.* So we can find some hope for humanity.

In a world increasingly obsessed with safety and security, we're losing grasp of a fundamental human need. Without human connection, we risk becoming trapped inside our own minds, locked inside our own prisons, spiraling out into mental illness until there's no turning back.

It's *all* about connection.

CHAPTER ONE

Beginnings

All my life, I've been following water. It started in the creek behind our Ohio family home, chasing crawdads, bluegills, box turtles. In high school, it was canoeing the Little Miami River with friends, chasing girls in bikinis. I caught one named Valerie and she became my wife. Together we explored the Big South Fork and Red River Gorge with backpacks, meandered the lakes of Kentucky and Tennessee by boat. Camping on the shores of small islands, we made love by moonlight, slept beneath a sea of stars.

As we ventured further west, water grew more sparse and intimate, yet no less enchanting. In Colorado, we found winding rivers, gurgling streams, sparkling alpine lakes. Wild rivers snaked across granite valleys. Kayaks splashed through whitewater canyons. In the red-rock deserts of Utah and Arizona, there appeared to be no water at all. But this was an illusion. Precious water trickled through deep canyons, hidden places of exquisite beauty and grandeur, tempting us to journey across miles of parched sand and bare rock—chasing holy water.

All my life, I've been wandering deserts, foothills, mountains, plains. Making my way home, back to the sea.

All comes from Mother Ocean, all returns to Mother Ocean. Each of us begins life in saltwater, the amniotic fluid in our mother's womb nearly identical to the sea. We hold the ocean in our veins, as the saline water in our cells is similar to seawater. The Earth is seventy percent water. Likewise, we are seventy percent water.

The similarities go on. The moon controls the rhythm of the great tides and the rhythms inside our own bodies—in ways beyond our understanding. Humans can go weeks without food, mere hours without water. It's all connected, and it all leads to the sea.

On a map, I can trace my route—from that childhood creek to this sandy shore by the Gulf of Mexico where I now write these words—and see my watercourse. Lakes, rivers, springs, seeps. Foothills, mountains, valleys, plains. Slowly making my journey back to the sea. Not a straight line, but a maze of undulating routes twisting and overlapping like the frantic doodling of a madman. The path is marked by water, a wild river flowing to the sea.

I feel as though I've been floating on a life raft, drifting with the Earth's currents. Where streams have diverged, I've taken obscure routes, drifting off into unknown territories. Along the way, I've encountered dry falls, choke stones, cliffs, dead ends. Places I've had to grasp for a rock, a root, a clump of tamarisk to pull myself onshore, fighting the current back, back, back to the last juncture. These diversions—right, wrong, or indifferent—have been my best teachers. If I've learned anything, it's that life is about taking risks. *Calculated* risks. When everything goes to shit, can I make it back to the last fork?

Mother Nature will carry you where she pleases. You may find salvation, you may find death. The trick is to *flow*—to navigate her natural rhythms like a bird on the wind, a surfer on a wave, a sailor on the open sea. There's a fine line between playing safe and playing smart. If you play it too safe, you risk reaching the destination but missing the journey. We're all headed for the same place. We all die. The difference is how we get there.

> *"...from the wavering edge of risk*
> *the sweetest honey of freedom drips."*
> —*Tom Robbins*

In a world where global and technological changes are occurring faster than ever, no one knows the future.

If there's anything we can count on, it's that the future is uncertain. Overpopulation, water shortages, air pollution, deforestation, chemical imbalances in nature—it seems we've reached the point of no return. As suicide rates fly high and more turn to alcohol and drugs, mental illness is slowly becoming the "new normal." It doesn't take a genius to see that old rules no longer apply.

How to plan for a future so unpredictable?

As much as we try to cling to the shore, the river of life flows. We forget that the ground beneath our feet is not steady but hurling through space at unfathomable speeds. With each passing year, the moon drifts further away, the Earth's rotation slows, and our days get progressively longer. As our climate warms, the oceans are advancing, coming back to reclaim the land—to wash away our sins.

Everything goes back to the sea.

Gloom and doom, or cause for celebration? When the world is ending, do we wallow in fear or have a party? I find it exciting that we get to witness such change in our lifetimes. Remember that Mother Nature ebbs and flows like the tides. It's all part of the Great Happening, and who are we to say it's not going perfectly as planned? If we could only step back, refocus, and see that we're not the main characters in the play. Not even supporting roles. In due time our buildings and houses, sidewalks and superhighways, strip malls and Walmarts will be brushed away—like dust from a rose. But the show...

The show goes on!

The world doesn't need saving. There is only saving ourselves. The *problem* is we've removed ourselves from the pulsing rhythms of life. Powerful technology has brought us to this unparalleled brink in time where Mother Nature barely recognizes us as her own. Looking down upon the Earth from outer space, we must look like aliens. An invasive species festering on the land.

Fortunately, there's a way back to nature, back to ourselves, if we learn to ride the tides— going *with* rather than against Mother Nature's currents. Only then might we hope to reclaim the status of Earthlings.

CHAPTER TWO

Headed for The Keys

The van is loaded with all the necessary equipment. Kayaks for paddling, masks and fins for snorkeling, a paddleboard for surfing, and my wing foiling gear (similar to windsurfing) for sailing. Simple, non-motorized vessels to help us connect with the ocean's elements: wind, water, and waves.

Valerie and I cross the border into the Sunshine State and stop for necessary provisions—beer and tequila—before heading south, then east on Alligator Alley through the swamps of the Everglades, and on toward that string of islands dangling off the southeastern tip of North America: the Florida Keys. On our map, they look like periods, commas, semi-colons. No possibility of a road. But as we know, a road indeed exists. U.S. Highway 1 is a rare spectacle of implausible engineering. Bridges up to seven miles long cross open expanses of water with panoramas in all directions. At times you can see the curvature of the Earth, thousand-hued waters blending seamlessly from sea to sky. Despite its close proximity to civilization, the place remains wild, exposed to storms, waves, the great rhythms of the tides. Like our mountains and deserts, the ocean rightfully demands our respect—a poignant mix of beauty and violence, tranquility and chaos.

It's September, the slowest time of the year. Summer is over and kids are back in school, but the snowbirds have yet to arrive. It's also hurricane season. This tropical chain of islands doesn't experience freezing weather, but it experiences storms—about two hurricanes a year. The season officially began back in June, but the biggest storms usually come in September, a sobering thought, considering our elevation is three feet above the sea. For every moment of calm, the ocean holds an equivalent of unrest. She is the ultimate metaphor for change.

Rambling south in our cargo van, we feel the local vibes downshift to a slower pace as we pass bait shops, harbors, marinas, tiki bars. Rolling down our windows, we let in the smells of the sea; salty air and conch fritters drift on the breeze.

The middle keys are wonderfully uncrowded, leaving the ocean pristine and untrammeled. The water immediately surrounding most of the islands is only a foot or two deep, far too shallow for the drafts of motorized boats. Occasionally we see flats fishermen poling the shallows, but for the most part, the water is undisturbed without ripple nor disturbance—except the occasional dorsal fin breaching the surface. Shark attacks are rare, killing about seven humans per year worldwide. Humans, on the other hand, kill a staggering 100 million sharks per year. Who experiences the greater threat?

Nonetheless, we're taught to fear sharks. Cars kill ninety humans per *day*, yet no one thinks twice about driving to the grocery store. Our fears are based on emotions rather than facts. Deep-seated emotions turn blind eyes to the truth, every chance they get.

The Keys are a regular paradise for aficionados of human-powered watercraft. And accessing the ocean is easy, with plenty of launches for small vessels like the ones we carry in our van. It's not just the lack of powerboats that draws us here, but also the quality of the water itself. Extreme clarity combined with shallowness transforms the water into a magnifying glass. There's often more to see below than above. With the balmy water temperatures hovering around 85 degrees, we'll spend as much time below the surface as above. Then there are the mangroves. Islands of twisted branches provide the perfect environment for the nesting and roosting of magnificent seabirds. For the ocean paddler, they offer endless wanderings. Tidal streams within these mangroves create tunnels through which one may navigate a maze of sea life. All is accessible simply by veering off the beaten path, away from U.S. Highway 1.

"There's nothin' down there 'til ya get to Key West…"

We heard this again and again, discussing our plan with strangers along the way. The typical tourist races through the Keys on their way to Key West, which is great for bar hopping or strolling in and out of tourist shops, but we're headed for the *nothin'* part. When people say there's nothing there, what they're referring to is tourist attractions. While U.S. Highway 1 is lined with businesses, the islands themselves are mere slivers of land, surrounded on all sides by open ocean—specks of dust on blue canvas. What lies beyond is an underwater wilderness dwarfing even the world's most expansive mountain ranges.

On one side of the highway, we have the Atlantic Ocean extending 41 million square miles to the east. On the other side, we have the warm, tranquil waters of the Gulf of Mexico. This relatively shallow ocean basin may appear placid, but it's anything but stagnant. Beneath the surface flows an ocean current 500 times the size of the Amazon River. From here to the Norwegian Sea, the powerful Gulf Stream makes its great northern journey, warming climates as far as Iceland. These nutrient-rich waters contain plant-like organisms called phytoplankton, which, besides supporting marine life, produce more than half the oxygen in the Earth's atmosphere. To this river of life, we owe our very existence. Without this valuable oxygen, we could not survive.

The ocean is the last great unknown, as more humans have visited the moon than the deepest parts of the sea. It's our largest natural habitat, covering over half the planet with an average water depth of two miles. It baffles and infuriates scientists because so little has been explored. Though much of the ocean's underwater landscape remains uncharted, it is full of life—including the largest animals ever to have roamed the Earth. Our oceans are home to the 16-foot manta ray, the 60-foot colossal squid, and the 110-foot blue whale that weighs as much as 200 tons. Twice the weight of the largest known dinosaur! Along the ocean floor, rolling plains, hidden canyons, and vast mountain ranges stretch out over 40,000 miles. Unlike our busy National Parks, these underwater wilderness areas receive few human visitors. Their inhabitants are as oblivious to our world as we are to theirs.

Just before sundown, we pull into a small harbor near Marathon, where we'll be housesitting for a friend—a *snowbird,* who winters in the Keys and spends her summers up north. Like many vacation homes, hers sits empty most of the year. She's allowing us to stay here for free in exchange for watching the place and doing general upkeep during our stay. These types of housing arrangements have helped support my writing career, allowing us the freedom to travel on a shoestring budget. A symbiotic relationship we are immensely grateful for.

When we exit the van, a sudden blast of humidity greets us, quickly followed by the heady smell of ganja drifting on the breeze. We are steps from a small marina with a tiki bar and a live band. After unpacking, we stroll over to the bar and order a couple of cold ones. Apparently, the marina is the local hangout for a small sailboat community in the harbor. Not vacationers, these are full-time live-aboards. People who washed in with the tides, dropped sail, never left. Perhaps they needed an escape—a place to lick their wounds and start a new life.

The old dock creaks and groans with dinghies and rowboats. Sailboats languish at their moorings in the sparkling bay. Happy hour has begun and the band is swinging, playing covers by the likes of Bob Seger, The Grateful Dead, Jimmy Buffett. The place oozes with laid back attitudes, a trademark of the Keys. We throw back a couple more beers, rekindling that pleasant feeling of being in the right place at the right time. It's easy to see that life is simple here. Time goes slowly. Days drift by without names. Our bartender arrives with coconut shrimp and conch fritters, and we waste away a perfectly good evening—lollygagging at the edge of the world.

CHAPTER THREE

Toptree Hammock

The next morning we allow ample time for coffee to extinguish last night's libations. After fixing breakfast, we load up the van. Our plan for the day is to head further south toward the island of Toptree Hammock, our first kayaking destination. We start off down the highway, again on U.S. 1, before veering off the main drag onto a bumpy road that quickly turns to sand. A mile further, we come to the water's edge: Land's End. When we shut off the engine, the first thing we notice is the absence of traffic noise. Only the ocean breeze and a few fish jumping in the bay. The air is thick with brine and stewing seagrass. Humidity mists our skin as we walk onto the hard sand, smooth and rippled from the outgoing tide. A maze of islands dots the horizon. No one else is here.

We unload kayaks, paddles, and assorted gear onto the beach. After lathering up with sunscreen, we slide our boats into foot-deep water. Luckily our small crafts draw only six inches and we glide effortlessly through water clear as crystal. We slide across the seagrass flats flickering with brilliant shades of green and yellow, the first group of islands growing closer with each stroke. There are no houses, no cars, no other boats in sight. Nothing but sea, sand, and sky.

A thriving community of loggerhead, vase, and column sea sponges immediately transfixes our eyes on the ocean floor. The strange shapes look like moldy brains, knobby truck tires, underwater volcanoes. I feel giddy, like a child at Disney World. This is what I live for, this feeling of experiencing something new.

We hover motionless over the swaying seagrass, absorbing their serenity. The day is hot and breathless. Peaceful silence surrounds us as we drift through the bay. Still hypnotized by the sponges, Valerie shrieks when she floats over a sleeping bonnethead. The hammerhead-like shark spooks and quickly darts from under her, dorsal fin slashing the surface, leaving the tiniest of wakes.

From rocky hideouts, spiny lobsters peek their antennas; loggerhead turtles paddle languidly between us—no ripples, no sound. We reach the mangroves and find them teeming with life. Hundreds of these uninhabited islands sprawl across the inland bays. Mangroves are the only trees that can survive in saltwater. Their twisted and overlapping roots help protect coastlines from waves and storms. In trapping sediment, they create small "bird islands," as Valerie and I like to call them, providing the perfect environment for herons, egrets, ospreys, bald eagles. The islands provide a steady diet of crab, shrimp, lobster, snapper, and an array of algae for the birds to feast on. A regular seafood buffet for the local wildlife.

Strange-looking jellyfish float through reflections of the clouds above. In the patches of sunlight, unidentifiable creatures flicker. The ocean clicks, rattles, gasps—silent messages bubbling from a hidden underworld we desperately wish to understand.

There's something about being at the edge of things. The jump-off point. Areas such as Hanksville, Utah. Stanley, Idaho. Joseph, Oregon. Places with exits from society. I get claustrophobic in cities that have no escape. With no access to wilderness, we create concrete prisons, boxing ourselves in from all sides. At the edge of civilization, I'm reminded of my true place in the world. I have my bearings. Gazing over huge expanses of mountains, deserts, or oceans, I couldn't give a damn about money or status or possessions. True wealth comes from freedom. I'll clean toilets for a living—so long as I'm free to climb mountains, explore canyons, paddle oceans.

The Keys themselves are far from true wilderness. Much of the land is covered with businesses and private homes. Yet the sea absorbs and pacifies this urbanized landscape. The eyes have something to fix on and the sun has a place to sleep. Despite its close proximity to civilization, the ocean remains wild. Gazing out over that great blue expanse, my imagination stirs. The sea is what this place is all about. That's why we've come.

Contrary to popular belief, you don't have to make a lot of money to live by the sea. Most of my friends that live near the coast are musicians, bartenders, service people. They find a way to make it work. I'm no millionaire, either. I'm certainly open to the idea if that should happen. But what then? Trade in my paddleboard for a yacht? My cargo van for a Hummer?

Happiness is wanting what you *have.*

Happiness comes in all sorts of flavors. It has little to do with money, fame, or success. Do what makes you happy and inevitably, you'll become a happy person. Do what makes you miserable, and a miserable person you become. The formula is simple. Unfortunately, our lives get so complex we forget about the simple things. The important things.

That's why I love the ocean. When I set my gaze to the open sea, it's just the rising and falling of the sun, the reflection of the moon on a clear night, the dolphins and seabirds, the waves that keep coming in day after day, year after year, century after century. It's all so simple, and so incredibly important, and there's absolutely nothing I can do about it.

That's the beauty of the whole thing—it happens without thinking. Like my breathing. The beating of my own heart.

We get so caught up in the details of everyday life. It's no wonder we're all on anxiety medicine. Most can't see the forest for the trees—because they've removed themselves from nature completely, or they're only focused on what can be extracted for profit.

Mother Nature provides the great power of perspective, helping us realize the futility of our efforts. For even if we succeed, we fail. We die, but the Earth lives on. She exists with or without us.

And so, if our efforts are futile, what do we do with our time here? This is the million-dollar question.

A group of pelicans soars above our heads. A pod of dolphins plays in the shallows...

Isn't the point to have fun? Isn't that the whole point and nothing but the point? Shouldn't we be spending our days celebrating the unfathomable notion that somehow we get to be humans in this whole shebang? How uncanny that we woke up today as people? The whole thing is ridiculous—like waking up one morning and realizing you're a zebra, or a penguin, or a giraffe. As *Homo sapiens*, we can surf and sail and dance and bake pastries. We can create art and play music and write poetry. The possibilities are endless! The candy bowl is full—choose a flavor.

In the heat of the sun, the sea caramelizes and the afternoon air grows heavy. We paddle laboriously toward the shore. Our arms ache, our stomachs rumble, our hearts brim with the freedom that comes only from a day spent on the sea.

CHAPTER FOUR

Curry Hammock

A few miles north of Marathon sits Curry Hammock, another island named for the shady, tropical hardwood hammocks that abound in the area. Dark brown mahogany. Olive-green lignum vitae. Reddish-colored gumbo limbo with peeling bark that resembles the sunburned skin of a tourist. And dark-chocolate colored poisonwood that produces an irritant similar to poison oak. If the sharks aren't enough to keep you away, the poisonous trees just might. But there is much to see beneath the hammock forests. Dripping ferns, voluptuous orchids, orange bromeliads with sword-like leaves. There are exotic butterflies, serenading songbirds, and white-crowned pigeons with striking yellow eyes. These tropical birds journey long distances over open water to dine on fruit trees that abound in the Keys.

On a low-tide morning, we drag our kayaks across wet sand and into the Gulf, casting off into open water. The ocean is still, the winds calm. Sweat drips from our chins as we paddle into the blinding sea. In the distance, small islands rise slowly from greenish blue waters. Thousands of mangroves stretch from here to the Everglades. Protected by the Florida Keys National Marine Sanctuary, the Great White-Heron National Wildlife Refuge, and the Key West National Wildlife Refuge, the mangroves are vital to wildlife in the Keys.

Fins to the left. Fins to the right. Sharks? Tarpon? We can't be sure, but they seem to be feeding on schools of baitfish under our hulls. In the corner of my vision, there's a flash. I twist around as a great mackerel falls out of the sky, splashing into the sea, flinging its spray toward our kayaks.

We are infatuated with solitary spaces. This landscape, where the land meets the sea, is musical, poetic. A place where you can feel the beat of the Earth, the pull of the moon, the mystery of the deep waters that cover most of our planet. A great whirring of life surrounds—above and below the surface.

Beneath our hulls, magnificent creatures stream past, the water so translucent we easily see everything that moves. Jellyfish with long tentacles, ancient-looking sea turtles, alien-like horseshoe crabs. From the vantage of our vessels, we have 360-degree views above, to the sides, and below—as if we're hovering weightless in the atmosphere. Drifting over deeper waters, I occasionally experience a strange sort of vertigo—like when peering over a tall building or steep cliff. The ocean floor is a loooong way down. A great egret flies above our heads, momentarily blocking the sun. His five-foot wingspan gives him the air of a prehistoric avatar.

A breeze spikes up, ruffling the surface as we cross an oystery rock bar and drift into the first group of mangroves. Soon we're entangled in a maze of narrow channels covered by thick canopies of twisted branches and salt-rimmed leaves. Colorful crabs and sea snails prowl the roots. Herons and ibises cling to insufficient branches, swaying with impeccable balance—silent, hunting.

The mangroves close in tightly, slowing our progress to a crawl as we continue through narrowing tunnels. We take a right fork, then a left. Each time it splits we take the widest opening— the path of least resistance. A quiver runs down my spine as a spider-like tree crab dangles an inch from my face. We press on with the tiniest of paddle strokes, occasionally pulling ourselves along with branches. There must be an opening in this jungle soon.

We enter a sunlit lagoon and pause for a few minutes in this shallow body of water enclosed within the mangroves. With outstretched arms, we gaze up into the blazing inferno above our heads, grateful for a momentary glimpse of open sky.

Branches creak, tree crabs click, spoonbills flutter. The wind has died and the heat is fierce. Sweat collects on my brow, droplets form and run down into my eyes. We desperately want to jump in to cool off, but the lagoon is far too shallow and tangled with roots, so we head back for the tunnels. Soon a wooden bridge appears as the familiar sound of traffic noise cracks into the hot silence, reminding us civilization is not far off. Minutes later, we're back in the open bay. It appears we've accomplished some sort of obscure loop, or figure eight, or pretzel. We couldn't have gone more than a couple of miles, but it feels like we've been outside for hours—like some time warp. That's the magic of mangroves. There's no destination but the islands themselves. They can swallow you up, take you into their world, show you things. They'll make you forget time and space. Then, just when you're sure you're completely lost, they'll spit you back out through a portal—back to your world. A curious blend of illusion and reality.

Nature is full of poetry and metaphor. Her wisdom is as necessary to our understanding of the world as science. There's always something new to comprehend—beyond facts, labels, charts. Things you can only see with the mind's eye. Those who spend countless hours outdoors will understand well enough what I mean. In Mother Nature's classroom we are permitted to remain children all our lives—for she can only be imperfectly comprehended. The more we learn, the more we realize how little we truly understand.

CHAPTER FIVE

Bahia Honda

The morning sun burns the sky clear of clouds while we drag our kayaks through the deep, powdery sand of Loggerhead Beach. As we slide our boats into the water, a light chop confuses the surface as we paddle out into open seas, beginning our circumnavigation of Bahia Honda Key.

When I think about the Keys, I don't envision land. What I picture is water. The thousand-hued waters surrounding Bahia Honda is usually the image I conjure. The entire southern shore of the island is lined with primitive white-sand beaches, swaying palms, and Caribbean-blue water. Perfect for paddling, snorkeling, swimming, lollygagging to your heart's content. Panoramic views of the Gulf and the Atlantic Ocean abound.

The horizon goes wobbly as an easterly gale spikes across the water. Progress slows in the headwind, taking a toll on our arms and shoulders. Soon we are paddling flat-out, hair streaming back in the wind when three dolphins surface right next to us. They are diving in unison, the morning sun glossing their backs. Unhurried and seemingly in slow motion, they swim alongside us for a while before tilting off into the beyond of deeper waters, tails swinging happily toward the abyss below.

We press on, straining our muscles now fatigued from many days of paddling. A seaplane groans low above our heads, flattening the choppy water, its shadow racing behind to keep up. We paddle harder, hugging the coast as we work toward the tip of the island. We round the bend, reaching the opposite shore where we can finally rest.

Now we drift *with* the wind.

Eager for a swim, we stow our paddles inside our boats and float with the breeze. Valerie jumps in, tethered with a surfboard leash to her kayak. I follow her, splashing in with my mask and snorkel. The water is bathtub-warm under the turquoise skies, and we drift lazily with the current. Grinning through gin-clear water, we giggle at the setting's splendor. I dive to the bottom and find pink shrimp, blue crabs, multi-colored conchs hiding in the seagrass. A stingray emerges beneath me in an explosion of sand, fluttering from his hiding place as I approach. I holler inhuman sounds through my snorkel, watching him race between my legs along the ocean floor. Mollusks and strange crustaceans consume every ounce of my attention until the pressure in my lungs is too much to bear. I dart to the surface, reminded again I'm just a visitor here. Human swimmers operate on borrowed time. Sooner or later, you have to breathe.

I climb aboard my kayak to catch up with Valerie. We're both hungry and head for shore. Parking our kayaks on a deserted beach, we rest in the shade of coconut palms. We dine on apples and almonds, followed by a nap under the rattling leaves for an undetermined amount of time...

Our species has become overwhelmed, exhausted, overstimulated—everyone is in a hurry to get nowhere. We've spent so much time within insulated structures that we've unplugged ourselves from the Earth's healing properties. The ocean has the great power to absorb negative energy and reground us. No special meditation techniques required. When I finally get to walk barefoot across hot sand and put my toes in water, I feel something. Something primal. I'm revitalized because when I reconnect to the Earth, a normalization begins. I can actually *feel* negative energy drain from my body. I've had great epiphanies while walking barefoot in the desert, on the beach, and in the mountains. Throughout all my writings, I've been directly connected to Mother Earth.

You may wonder what a desert rat is doing in the Florida Keys. We're a long way from the mountains and deserts detailed in my other nature books. But the mother of all wildernesses sits at my doorstep. "The last great frontier," as Rachel Carson called it. The one true wilderness—from which all life comes and shall return: Mother Ocean.

My parents first brought me here as a child. I met Valerie in these islands. And they are where she last saw her father before he passed. Our families have been coming here for decades. This place holds magic. So we've come back to celebrate love, life, freedom—at the edge of the world.

In the haze of the afternoon, we wake from our tropical siesta and paddle back to Loggerhead Beach, drifting on the wind. Before leaving the island, I stop in at the Bahia Honda State Park office and arrange for a boat ride out to Looe Key Reef the following day. Looe Key is part of a two-hundred-mile-long reef system that runs parallel to the Keys. Located ten miles offshore, it's too far for us to safely paddle.

Looe Key is a wildlife sanctuary for parrotfish, barracuda, butterflyfish, angelfish, spotted eagle rays, and nurse sharks, just to name a few sea creatures. Dubbed the "rainforests of the seas," these ocean reefs are fragile pieces of rare beauty that take thousands of years to build. They are a haven for over 650 species of tropical fish and an absolute gem for snorkeling.

The next morning, we awake to the now-familiar sounds of boats tugging at their moorings. The wind is calm, the sea flat and shimmering. A perfect day for snorkeling. After fixing coffee and breakfast, we climb into the van and head out across Seven Mile Bridge. This has become our daily commute: rolling down the highway, the ocean stretching far and wide, searching for freedom, adventure, fun.

When we reach Bahia Honda, we find our boat and captain waiting as planned. He's sun-bronzed, shirtless, probably in his twenties. Not a bad gig, shuttling folks around to coral reefs in the Keys. I'm continually amazed by how many ways one can make a living in this great country. When everything is ready, we set out, racing toward the sunrise as we head off into open waters. A few dolphins surf our wake as we hold onto the rails, skating across a motionless sea. These dolphin sightings have become regular occurrences, yet we never take them for granted. Now having observed them daily, I can easily understand why these playful mammals took to the sea.

Alongside our boat, a dozen needlefish race across the surface, running on the tips of their tails, apparently chased by larger predators below. Twenty minutes later, our boat makes a large arc, then angles toward some mooring balls signifying Looe Key Reef. The captain kills the motor; looking down, we already see the multi-colored reef. A few rainbow parrotfish hover above the corals, casually glancing back at us with nonchalance.

It doesn't take long for us to slip into masks, snorkels, and fins, splashing together into the aqua-blue water. Instantly, we're engulfed by colorful fish. Parrotfish, butterflyfish, blueheads, trumpets, yellowtail snapper. Valerie and I hold hands, floating calmly amongst the fish, absorbing the surreal scene into every fiber of our beings. We've snorkeled in Mexico, Costa Rica, Hawaii, and still, we're never prepared for the magnificence that exists around these natural coral reefs.

The corals themselves are built by tiny animals called polyps which need sunlight to survive. Because water near the coast is shallow, light penetrates to the bottom, generating nutrients that support the basis of the oceanic food chain. Fish around the reefs are cloaked in the most exotic attires, from velvety purple and fiery red to blazing yellow and sapphire blue. Nothing stirs the imagination and tantalizes the senses quite like snorkeling.

I practice my freediving skills—swimming deep while withstanding the mounting pressure in my ears, the burning expression in my chest. The calmer my mind, the longer I'm able stay. Up close and personal, I inspect a blue parrotfish chomping off a chunk of coral with his powerful beak. Later he'll eject the particles into a fine white powder that creates the white sand beaches around the Keys. That beautiful white sand under your towel? That's right. Parrotfish poop.

I resurface for air, then quickly dive back down as a table-sized eagle ray comes into view. Relatives of sharks, stingrays hunt by detecting tiny electrical pulses given off by the muscle activity of clams, mussels, and small fish. Flapping his muscular pectoral wings, he glides across the ocean floor like a great underwater bird of prey.

A six-foot nurse shark sleeps peacefully on the bottom. Though characteristically slow and sedentary, these sharks can and do bite, ranking fourth in attacks among humans. I keep a respectful distance, not wishing to disrupt her ocean slumber. We show the same respect for the jellyfish, though find it impossible not to be mesmerized by their electrical currents flashing pink, silver, green, blue. Interestingly enough, turtles eat them. Their stomach linings must be made of iron.

Sunlight beams through the water, infusing the scene with theatrical ambiance as the morning evolves. Each time we spy something new, we point and grin around our snorkels, shrieking underwater delights back and forth. I feel like we're diving through a movie set, everything big and in Technicolor, vivid and dramatic. Plankton spins before our eyes, currents root through our hair, and we kick lazily through the reefs. Time turns elastic. The peacefulness down here, it's religious. I feel like we could live here. Stay here. Die here. A warm, dreamless sleep.

I turn to Valerie, her bikini bright and blue, her skin radiant, her hair swaying in flickers of light.

We join hands in underwater silence, letting this dreamy haze of a life we've created together wash over us. It's our 25th wedding anniversary. Holy moments, these are. Ones we'll remember while sitting in retirement rockers on some front porch in who-knows-where.

CHAPTER SIX

Paddleboarding

Each morning I wake in the dark, sit on the veranda, and listen to the owls. From the harbor, I gaze over the bay. This time of morning is drenched in stillness, disrupted only occasionally by the splashing of fish. In the bay, submerged lights cast shadows that flash and flicker. Large fish pass before the glow, blocking out the light like an underwater eclipse.

Clouds gather on the eastern horizon. A stiff breeze rattles the palms, sending ripples across the harbor. The sunrise begins in slow-motion explosions of pink, purple, orange—rising up, up, up through the clouds until finally bursting through, blasting me with yellow light. I set down my journal, sip the last of my coffee, then make my way to the harbor. Near the docks is a shed where residents stow their gear—fishing poles, kayaks, paddleboards, other water toys. The room is dark and damp and smells of the sea. I'm giddy inside this adult toy box: I can choose my own adventure, my vessel for freedom and fun. Outside the door are gateways to the great salty wilderness that surrounds the islands. There's so much to explore, and it all starts here.

When tides are high, I launch my paddleboard from the docks and point toward a maze of mangrove islands right off the harbor. The place is filled with sea life, enticing me to wander slowly, pausing often to witness rare and precious wonders. A stunning array of seabirds crowd the mangroves. Pelicans, cormorants, ibis. Herons, hawks, bald eagles. And the flamboyant roseate spoonbill, which looks like a pink flamingo. Dolphins, manatees, sheepshead, and mangrove snapper roam the shallows. But when tides are low, this passage is difficult—my fin could easily catch the bottom and throw me onto beds of sharp oyster shells. On these days, I carry my board across the street where the Gulf stretches far and wide. The beach is pristine with turquoise water, soft sand, and all of civilization to my back. This is my choice today, as tides are low and the Gulf shimmers.

The paddleboard is a simple vessel, like the earliest of boats, which began as nothing more than a wooden plank and a single pole. My modern version is beautifully shaped fiberglass, which glides effort-lessly on water, providing a high vantage point to observe every fish, every rock, every piece of coral living below.

I paddle through the shallows, past sandbars, through flashing schools of baitfish. The Gulf is thick with thousands of them, darting from my approach as I slice through their wild fury. When I drift into deeper waters, the schools disappear, leaving only sea and sky. Down shore toward the reefs, the southern horizon is blinding. A sea turtle breaches the surface. Slowly, I move toward him and we paddle together until I mistakenly call out, "Good morning, my ocean friend!" He spooks, diving into the deep.

I paddle down the coast for another ten minutes, eyes fixed on the horizon, the unblemished sea, before noticing the unmistakable bubbles of a manatee producing boils and odd swirls on the surface. She comes close and we travel together a long while. Moving slowly as manatees do, she matches the cadence of my paddle stroke. With a respectful distance between us, we travel side by side, two worlds briefly merging into one. Every so often, she lifts up for air, her sleek body rising gracefully from the water until her tail completes the arc, breaking the surface with a splash. She's nine feet long, probably a thousand pounds. Graceful, docile, ancient. I've paddled alongside manatees more times than I can count yet the experience of awe, reverence, respect, and admiration never dulls. I treasure these sacred experiences with wild animals.

With no motor, I glide silently along, leaving the marine life in peace below. At any moment, I could jump in for a swim—or sit and let baitfish nibble at my toes. Sometimes I lie down and close my eyes. Or gaze up at the open sky. The open ocean: there's nothing like being out here, rising and falling with the rhythms of her rolling swells, only the sounds of the gulls, the smell of saltwater.

I paddle parallel to the coast, about a half mile from shore, removed from the sounds of human activity—on the edge of things—that fine line between freedom and security—that perfect ratio of safety and risk. Each time I venture out, my muscles become stronger, my competence levels more proficient. When weather changes, as it often does, I've developed the skills to return safely to land. When a distant storm stirs the sea, I'm filled with adrenaline rather than fear, longing for a good wave to ride to shore.

Each morning I check weather reports to see when the winds are predicted to change. If I time things right, I can paddle down the coast with the wind to my back, then return when it shifts, with the wind at my back again. However, no one can fully rely upon these forecasts. At any point, I may have to battle stiff headwinds on my way back. If the gales grow too fierce, I must lie down on my stomach and paddle with my arms—prone style—reducing wind resistance as I voyage home. If all else fails, I'll do the "walk of shame," trudging down the beach, lugging my board under my arm. But all the while, I'm conditioning, honing my abilities and becoming a better waterman. Every day I feel more connected to the sea.

Mother Ocean is a great healer. When things get crazy, I simply jump into the ocean, and my land-locked problems disappear. It's just me and the sea. My body softens as I become yielding and flexible like water itself. Anxieties are washed clean, and every cell is tuned to the sea. It's a process of forgetting while also remembering what's truly important. The dolphins, manatees, rays, and sea turtles are all the companions I need. My world feels right again.

I am both sociable and reclusive. In solitude, I connect with my eternal nature and face my human mortality. Yet, when facing my mortality, I crave human connection. This oscillation sends me to the ethers, then keeps me coming back. Going to the mountains usually entails organizing, then driving, then hiking miles into a forest with a heavy pack. Here, I simply paddle into the ocean. I'm less than a mile from civilization yet feel a world away.

The ocean holds the great power of transformation. I feel it the moment I leave the shore and become weightless, floating. With civilization to my back, the magnitude of the ocean wilderness before me is so powerful, so consuming, that I'm forced into present-moment awareness. Every movement, every paddle stroke, every shift in balance feels crucial. No longer am I traveling *toward* mindfulness. I'm in it from the start. My brain switches gears from scattered to laser focused. I become an animal, scanning the horizon for movement and sudden changes, keeping a watchful eye for predator or prey. My mind becomes meditative—peaceful, yet alert, ready for whatever might come from the water. Each time I go out, I'm surprised by what I find.

One day I glide over a pod of a hundred stingrays. On another occasion I find myself surrounded by sharks, their fins slashing the surface in some feeding frenzy. I've seen sea turtles mating and baby dolphins doing the backstroke. Often I'll carry snorkeling gear, so when the mood strikes, I can explore the sparkling sunlit waters below. There, every ounce of attention is consumed— schools of colorful fish surround me, curious crustaceans creep out from rocks, saltwater seeps into my pores, my body undulates with the ocean's currents, and for a while, I become a sea creature myself.

The spectacular vitality of the sea ignites my own. Senses come alive—the whooshing crash of waves, the salt-crusted air, the rocking of my body, rising and falling with rolling swells. Great peace descends as her waves lull me back to life, recalibrating my internal rhythms. I become formless, shapeless like the sea. All the while, I'm exercising balance, honing intuition, cultivating awareness. Epiphanies rain down a mile a minute.

The mood swings of Mother Ocean are wild and varied like my own, changing with the seasons, the weather, the tides. Rather than isolation out here, I sense oneness—I no longer feel like a drop in the ocean—I'm the entire ocean in a drop! My heartbeat steadies, my breathing relaxes. I feel the ocean flowing through my veins, the saltwater in my tears.

This transcendence can occur daily on the sea. To reach this degree of confidence, it takes time and effort, yet with practice, it becomes second nature: I now move through my saltwater environment with style and grace, harnessing her pules and rhythms as opposed to fighting her currents. This practice bleeds into my terrestrial life, inviting me to live more intentionally, with less anxiety. I move slower and more deliberately even through the mundane tasks of cleaning gear, taking a shower, washing the dishes. Flowing with nature's currents, we evolve into happier people. We develop better relationships, we do better work, we raise better families. We become better Earthlings.

Afternoons consist of riding beach bikes into the village, where the conversation is easy and strangers quickly become friends. Everyone has one thing in common: We all feel lucky. We're happy to be here. Happy to be alive.

I've been to dreary towns where people are happy. I've been to drop-dead-gorgeous towns where people are miserable. You see it in their eyes, that blank stare from way inside their heads. What causes people and places to lose their magic? Times change, people change, the economy changes—I get it. These things are inevitable. But stay too long in these places and they'll suck you in, become part of your identity. Misery is contagious. Sometimes to get somewhere you have to *go* somewhere. Maybe with only the clothes on your back. Sometimes we must pull in the anchor, leave the harbor, cast off into unknown seas.

If I belong anywhere, it's among the likes of dirt-bags, surfers, nomads, desert rats. Seeking truth in faraway places, forever chasing vista and sunset, longing to gaze into the eye of the storm, sail off the edge of the world. Nothing is more beautiful than truth. Truth is poetry.

Under a fish scale sky, I paddle into a rolling swell. Storm clouds build on the horizon, isolated flashes, distant thunder. The water turns black as oil. Rising and falling to the heartbeat of the sea, I move past empty beaches, paddling toward the rain, anticipating it, welcoming it. It's midsummer and the water is too warm to cool you off. I've spent the entire afternoon playing and surfing with dolphins. During these brief off-season periods, the porpoise are everywhere, grateful to have the coast to themselves. The farther I go, the darker the sky. I can't bring myself to leave the sea.

Rain comes. Heavy and ferocious, turning the water to dimples. I reach my arms up into the sky and the cool liquid runs through my hair, down my face, my chest, a delightful respite from the midday heat. No other humans out here today. Just me and the porpoise. The swell intensifies, producing a set of surfable waves, and we ride together again, porpoise and human. Me atop the wave, the dolphins inside it. They spin and play, shooting me gleeful glances as we surf—rare, sacred moments of joy with these wild animals.

In a storm, the sea can be a harsh, unforgiving place. But these drops fall straight down out of the sky. The waves are smooth, textured now only by raindrops. At the edge of my vision, a silvery flash. A tarpon breaks the surface, splashing back into the water with an awkward smack. Further in the distance, a six-foot eagle ray emerges, black as ink, flapping his dripping muscular wings in the air as if attempting to fly. And then, three feet from my board, the wrinkled, ancient head of a sea turtle.

He ponders me for a moment before diving back into the hidden sea. The ocean teems, alive with life.

A wave barrels toward me. I'm right in the take-off zone. I paddle hard as it approaches, arrive at its crest and slide down its smooth, curling face. I'm a novice surfer and these are relatively small waves, but my ten-foot paddleboard can ride just about anything. I surf down the beach before the sea dumps me in her froth, setting off the usual flailing of arms, underwater somersaults, burning lungs. But I've gotten used to the falling—it's a necessity of the sport. As I tumble through the chaos, I merge with it momentarily, find rhythm within it. I've learned to protect my face and head with my arms until I'm discharged, usually near shore. Immediately, the urge strikes again: Paddle back out. Surf another wave. Fight through the impact zone. Reach that magical place where the sea is smooth and glassy. But I've already been out for hours. My arms ache, my skin is tight, my hair a tangled mess of salt and sand. I call it a day and swim back toward hot food and a frosty beer.

CHAPTER SEVEN

Gilligan's Island

On Saturdays, we go to church. There's this bar called Gilligan's where the same band plays every week and the regular crowd hasn't changed in decades. The place is full of outlaws, outcasts, musicians, people who live by their own rules. They've all somehow coalesced here at the edge of the world. On Saturdays, we celebrate our colorful coexistence.

The place rings with laughter and music. Everyone is eager to meet a new face, strike up a conversation with a stranger. Bad vibes don't exist. One of the old-school locals makes sure of it. Everyone calls him "The Mayor." If anyone gets unruly, he walks over with the biggest grin you've ever seen, politely puts his arm around them, then walks them outside. We all love The Mayor.

Marijuana smoke drifts through the back door as the band returns from set break. The bassist tunes a string. The drummer suggests a beat. The guitarist strums a melody and it flows softly, patiently into song. When the singer puts his mouth to the microphone, he points his words right at you, filling your soul with passion and emotion. Through the bar, sunlight angles in, reflecting off guitar strings, drum kits, microphone stands.

One local tells me he sleeps in an RV, parks it on the street, no one minds. Another lives on the boat he inherited from a former employer. Must have been a good worker. Everyone is a character with a story to tell. Semi-true stories, like Jimmy Buffett's songs. Such is life in the tropics. I could write an entire book about the history of this bar, call it *Life According To Gilligan*.

Oh, the stories it could tell...

Everyone knows everyone, yet the vibe is not cliquey. Old-timers and newcomers are greeted with friendly smiles, nods, raised glasses. It's welcome one, welcome all. So long as you're not a douchebag. That's the only rule here: "NO ASSHOLES," posted squarely behind the bar. Fine by me. I don't care who you are, who you fuck, who you vote for, or what god you pray to at night. Just don't be an asshole.

I'd like to start *that* religion.

> Asshole *(noun)*: A militant or hateful person. One who takes themselves far too seriously: the far left, the far right, the intolerant.

Another beer please...

The church music continues—melancholy, joyful, somber—sometimes all three in a single song, a single solo. We sing, we dance. We laugh, we cry. When the band finishes an especially poignant number, The Mayor struts up to the tip jar and bellows, "That's another five-dollar song!" tossing a five-spot into the jar. Everyone follows suit, we all cheer, and it's high fives and clinking glasses all around. The band makes bank. So does the bartender. She's worked here twenty years, calls everyone by name, makes us ornaments at Christmastime, buys us beers on our birthdays.

Saturdays at Gilligan's. Everyone calls it family day because it is.

CHAPTER EIGHT

Changes in Latitudes, Changes in Attitudes

You're from where? Colorado? Too cold for me!

We get this from the locals. Our Colorado friends said the same thing: *You're headed where? Florida? Too hot for me!* This casual chit-chat bounces between friends and strangers—we have strong opinions about the small worlds in which we reside. Neither view is *wrong*, each is simply biased due to limited scopes of experience. Anyone traveling to Florida dressed for Colorado will probably roast.

Anyone traveling to Colorado dressed for the tropics will likely freeze. Any climate can be comfortable or miserable depending on the circumstances.

I've sweat my ass off skiing in a snowstorm, shivered my ass off on a summer ferryboat ride. It all depends on how we're prepared for the circumstances. When we get used to certain climates, we adjust our habits. When it's summertime in the tropics, my best friend is a long-sleeved SPF shirt. It's like wearing air-conditioning, especially when wet. Fabric takes forever to dry in humidity, so I use that to my advantage. When the shirt finally dries, I remedy the situation by jumping into the ocean or dunking it in the nearest sink.

Mountains require layering. When it's cloudy in the summer, you can still feel chilly. When it's sunny in the winter, you can easily overheat. So you learn to adapt. This adaptability comes naturally in our youth. When we're young and unbiased, we want to experience all types of weather. When we get older, we form hard-edged opinions about climates, cultures, foods, everything.

I hate cats, says someone who's only owned dogs. *I'm not a water person*, says someone who's only lived in Arizona. Let's not forget that under different circumstances, our opinions could be entirely different. Take religion for example. Why do you think people who live in the Bible Belt share similar beliefs? Is it because each individual arrived at those ideas on their own? Or were their beliefs adopted from those around them? We know the answer.

If the people and environments surrounding us influence our beliefs, wouldn't it be natural to assume these beliefs are not entirely our own?

There's nothing wrong with thinking a certain way or holding certain beliefs—religious, political, cultural, or otherwise. What's important is that we don't take those beliefs too seriously. That's when everything goes to shit. We form hierarchies in our minds. We start arguments, fights, even wars based on what we think is *right*.

DO WHAT'S RIGHT!, we demand.

Meanwhile, the other person thinks they're also right. And that person could be you had your circumstances been different.

Remember when the goal of conversation was to try and understand the other person? When did we become so close-minded to new ideas? When did we become so quick to judge? When did the tides turn? Once we were so eager to learn, now we justify ways to shut those out with ideas that don't align with our own. Do we no longer have the capacity to love thy neighbor as thyself, regardless of their views?

Unity is *not* uniformity. Do we really want to become one nation, one religion, one political party, one race? Unity is about coexistence, the ability to say to all colorful beings: *I respect how you feel, even though I don't feel the same way.* Then you crack a beer and go fishing together. No one tries to change the other. This is coexistence. Unity.

Each of us is born with the capacity to love thy neighbor as thyself. Then at some point, we lose sight of it. Can we ever get back to our playful, childlike, trusting selves? How can we dissolve this incessant judging that contaminates our thoughts and behaviors?

It's simply impossible to judge someone else until you see their unique points of view, step into their shoes, feel their world. Each of us experiences reality through a different set of eyes, different circumstances. Your circumstances define who you are, my circumstances define who I am, and neither of us is wrong.

Does the liver know better than the stomach? Or does it do what it does best, allowing the stomach to do what it does best, thus benefiting the whole? Nature was designed to work this way harmoniously. Could it be any other way? Would we want it any other way?

It all goes back to Aladdin's lamp and the three wishes. Why the third wish? To get back to where you started after making a mess with the first two. When you expect others to change for your own selfish needs, you are, in effect, trying to play God, declaring the whole system flawed—asserting that *you* know best.

CHAPTER NINE

Non-Traditional Surfing

I've been a non-traditional surfer all my life. Concrete, dirt, water, snow—you name it, I've surfed it. Whether on a skateboard, mountain bike, paddleboard or skis, surfing is how I connect with the Earth's natural rhythms. I'm not much of a traditional surfer, but to me, surfing simply means dancing with Mother Nature.

Skateboarding taught me the fine art of flowing with gravity. Lifeless landscapes came alive when stale suburban features morphed into concrete waves. I surfed and danced and discovered that even under the worst of circumstances, I could be happy. Most of all, I could have fun.

Skateboarding had meaning. It was something I could learn from, practice, and evolve with. It connected me with my environment and with others who shared similar interests. It was a lifestyle, and it changed my life. I learned that no matter how bad external circumstances might be, I would always find a way to have fun.

In my thirties, I transitioned to mountain biking. Bikes are more expensive than skateboards, so I took a job at our local bike shop. As a bicycle mechanic, I learned the art of fine-tuning bikes to my exact preferences and specifications, so much they felt like extensions of my body. Mountain biking grounded me throughout stressful periods in my life. It kept me happy, healthy, and continually looking for new places to ride. It, too, was a lifestyle, connecting me with other riders, taking me on road trips, and imbuing my whole life with meaning. I think that's what we're searching for—something meaningful in our lives.

Next came snowboarding. Surfing snow. Dancing on diamonds! It started with ski resorts, but after a while, I grew tired of expensive lift tickets, long lines, and frozen chairlifts. I took a backcountry ski course in the Tetons and fell in love with climbing empty, wintery mountain ranges under my own power, skiing virgin powder instead of groomed runs. A whole new world opened up. Every snow-covered mountain range became an arena for freedom and fun. It gave my life direction, keeping me up at night, drooling over guidebooks, maps, glossy magazines. Dreaming of the next stoke.

These activities have defined my life. I've stayed in shape both mentally and physically, not because I want to, but because I *have* to. Destructive habits like overeating and drug abuse don't exist when all my decisions continuously point me toward the next stoke. The next *natural* high.

When we participate in meaningful activities, peace of mind comes naturally. But we must remain adaptable as our lives ebb and flow. I couldn't skateboard forever, just as a professional athlete can't play quarterback forever. When things become too difficult, or cause too many injuries, or we're no longer progressing, it's time to move on. Fortunately, the world is filled with meaningful activities—for every age and ability.

When Valerie and I planned our trip to Florida, I immediately searched for what activity I'd sink my teeth into. My first thought was surfing, but with water around this coast being mostly flat, I didn't want to be sitting around waiting for waves. Paddleboarding fit the bill perfectly, turning the ocean into my next arena of exploration. Instead of just gazing out to sea, I could walk on water. The mangrove-filled inland bays were just waiting to be explored. And when the storms came in, I could surf!

How could I ever be bored?

I have to be careful though. Things can easily backfire if I focus too much on the activity rather than where it *takes* me—a lesson I've learned a thousand times. I must constantly remind myself that these activities are simply vessels, connecting me with something much greater than the activity itself. If I make the vessel what I'm chasing, this easily becomes a trap. Suddenly it's all about winning or losing or getting the perfect score. The activity loses meaning and I lose sight of the greater voyage.

"A raft needed to cross the river
is discarded when the other shore is reached,
not carried about on one's head."
—Buddha

Our activities are like life rafts. We use them to navigate life. Some float on the musical notes of a piano. Others on the wings of an airplane, the sails of a schooner, or walking along high wires strung across skyscrapers. You may climb mountains, run marathons, race cars, perform heart transplants. You may take photographs, write books, play chess, bake pies. Our life rafts can be anything, even doing the dishes. Perhaps in any activity, we may find our Zen, our surfer's stoke, our runner's high. That place of no-mind that we all can experience when we're absorbed in the moment. That place where we flow like water, surf like dolphins, ebb and flow like the great tides.

We flail and flounder at the beginning of any new activity. But over time, we become skilled navigators of our chosen life rafts. Then, if we're lucky, we become masters. This is living at full throttle, as life was meant to be lived.

The secret to living a meaningful life?

Do something well. Really well. Look at nature and you'll find this to be true. Birds master the art of flying. Fish master the art of swimming. Plants master the art of flowering. You won't find a dolphin deliberating its life's purpose. It's to swim! The better swimmer she becomes, the more she gets to eat, the less chance she has of being eaten, and the more fun she gets to have being a dolphin. Humans no longer have this inherent sense of purpose. Our days of chasing food and running from predators are long behind us. The pursuit of fun has been relegated to our free time when we're finished doing more *important* things. Because of this, we no longer have a sole defini-tion of what it means to be human. There are just so many choices. This can be very exciting. It can also be quite terrifying. Many become paralyzed with indecision at the sheer vastness of possibility. Constantly, we're being persuaded to do this or do that, so much we rarely stop to ask ourselves what we actually *enjoy* doing.

The solution? Find something with deep personal meaning and do it exceptionally well. Do this and you will find your Zen, your surfer's stoke, your runner's high. Why blunder through life when you can fly like a bird, surf life like a dolphin, run like a gazelle? Each of us can master something, but we must enjoy what we're mastering. If we do it for money, fame, recognition, or because we feel pressured, then mastering becomes a burden. There's no joy in the journey because it's all about the destination. You might become proficient, but rarely will you find happiness.

When we develop new skills, we become like children again. New worlds open up as fresh landscapes emerge and we never see the world again in the same way. We need this refresh in our lives. Other animals live in this state of ecstasy all the time. A long time ago, we did too. Only recently have we confined ourselves to offices, desk chairs, computer screens. Humans were not designed to be stagnant. We are meant to surf and dance like other Earthlings.

Though the actual experience of ecstasy may be short-lived, it resonates deeply into the rest of our lives. Addictive? Certainly, but with what possible downside? Especially when it distracts us from so many other self-destructive behaviors.

We need something to escape from the mundane, shake us out of our skin, feel high for a while. We need to tune back into our natural state of ecstasy. We need to experience God.

For this reason, I surf.

The sooner I get down to surfing, the sooner I get down to dancing. And in this dancing, I see that the universe is one big happening. I look at the gulls and notice they, too, are dancing, as are the dolphins, the stingrays, the turtles, the jellyfish. This is life. We get up, we fall down, we get up, we fall down—just like ocean waves. The point is to keep dancing.

CHAPTER TEN

Wing Foiling

I learned wing foiling to dance with the wind. I've always wanted to sail, but a sailboat doesn't fit my lifestyle, and it certainly doesn't fit in the van. Perhaps someday I'll write a book about island hopping the Caribbean, but until then, I need a simpler vessel, something easily carried to the beach by hand. When things are calm, a paddleboard is great. But when winds pick up, they blow you all over. I needed a way to harness the wind. I needed to sail.

In my paddleboard magazines, I'd been reading about a new sport called wing foiling, also known as foiling or winging. Many consider it a combination of kiteboarding and windsurfing. However, the equipment is more compact, the learning curve is shorter, and there's the huge advantage of sailing in light winds. The activity entails holding a lightweight sail, or "wing," in your hands while standing on a small surfboard. Attached to the bottom of the surfboard is a hydrofoil, which is essentially a long fin connected to something that looks like a model airplane. At low speeds, the hydrofoil is submerged. As wind speeds increase, the hydrofoil creates lift—like an airplane—pushing the surfboard above the water. You essentially levitate. The feeling is something like snowboarding fresh powder. The wing easily collapses, stuffs into a backpack, and the whole apparatus weighs less than thirty pounds. With winging, instead of battling the wind, I could use it to my advantage. I could learn to fly.

I called a local shop for a lesson and agreed to meet them at a spot prime for beginners. My instructor was knowledgeable and patient, and after three hours, I was up and winging.

Well... barely. I could sail for a few seconds before crashing into the water, but I understood the concept. At least enough to practice on my own, or so I thought. At the end of the lesson, I was hooked. Like hooked in a bad way. I wanted to wing foil like nothing else.

The day the delivery man arrived with my own equipment, I was a kid again on Christmas morning. I had everything assembled quickly, ready to start my new adventure. Then came the part I didn't expect. The part I forget each time I start a new endeavor. The nervousness. The apprehensiveness. The wooziness in my stomach. What had I gotten myself into? Would I remember anything from the lesson? It had taken me hours to get up the first time, and that was with an instructor. What if I forget everything he taught me? What if I drown? What if I drift off to sea?

Valerie consoled my apprehension, agreeing to come spot me while I tried out my new sport... and to call the Coast Guard if I don't make it back to land.

Surprise: I didn't get lost at sea. But I also didn't make it out of the water and onto the hydrofoil. Not the first day. Not the second. Not even the third. I could feel Valerie eyeing me like I'd wasted our money on this silly contraption. But I was determined. I wanted to learn this sport more than anything else.

After floundering like a fish out of water for far too long, I finally hit the perfect day with steady offshore breezes and a shimmering sea. Fortunately, in my practice sessions, I'd learned the important skill of tacking, which entails zigzagging into the wind, so you can safely return to land in offshore breezes. I paddled into the glassy water, brilliant sunshine pounding my back. At first, the wind seemed absent, but the further from shore I got, the stronger it became. Once past the sandbars, I knelt on my board, raised the wing above my head, and let the wind carry me further out to sea. Then came the first big gust. Quickly, I stood up, positioned myself perpendicular to the breeze, and felt a sudden burst of speed. The wind took over completely as I pumped my wing a few times for extra power. And then... and then... I was flying.

To fully describe this feeling is impossible, but I'll do my best. The first thing you notice is the silence. Once on the hydrofoil, your board hovers above the choppy waters and drag resistance all but evaporates. There's nothing except the wind. Then comes a sudden boost of acceleration like an airplane lifting from a runway, then weightlessness takes over as you race across the open ocean. The speed alarmed me at first, so I de-powered the wing just a bit, adjusting my grip and holding it slightly more horizontal, rather than vertical, to the wind. Then slowly, I relaxed into this magical feeling of flying above the sea.

Twenty seconds later, I went crashing into the water. But it'd felt like forever. When I emerged, I could not contain my excitement and let out a great big *Woohooo!* No one was around to hear, save a couple of amused dolphins. It didn't matter. It felt like losing my virginity.

These early experiences of "getting it" are priceless. The feeling is electrifying. Remember riding your bike for the first time without training wheels? One of my earliest memories of "getting it" was learning to ollie—a skateboarding maneuver that allows you to jump over things and do tricks. I'd been trying for weeks in my parents' driveway, slapping down the tail of my skateboard awkwardly on the pavement, again and again, never leaving the ground. Then one day, something clicked. I got air. Just an inch at first, but it was air! From that moment forward, I had it. The next day I got two inches of air, then four. Soon I was clearing soda cans, paint buckets, milk jugs. I wanted to tell the world. Throw a party! The same thing happened when I learned to surf, and ski, and Eskimo roll my kayak. These were all gateways to exciting new worlds. New ways to dance. New ways to connect. New ways to live.

Whether figuring out how to talk to girls or studying to be an electrician, such early learning experiences are life-changing. Our lives can feel short because there's so much we want to accomplish, we just hope there's enough time to live our dreams. Full steam ahead, we charge into new and exciting worlds— worlds we've created for ourselves by following our passions, our joys, our curiosities. And that's just it—*we create them*. These experiences weren't given to us. They weren't handed down, nor did we stumble upon them by accident. We put in our time—learning, practicing, fumbling, making many mistakes—until we finally got it.

This is all very exciting initially. But the feeling diminishes over time as we get accustomed to our new skills. When we're nine months old, walking is the most exciting thing in the world. At 42, it's lost a bit of luster. And it's not that we shouldn't be grateful every day for our ability to walk—not everyone is so lucky—but it's simply not feasible to maintain the same level of enthusiasm forever. Therefore, we must keep reaching for the doors of new worlds through learning. When we become content with the skill sets required to live comfortable lives, we quit learning. That's when we become stagnant. It's just a matter of time before life begins to feel long.

When life begins to drag on, to where we think, *Is this all there is?*, we've reached the end of the road by exhausting our skill sets. The solution here is simple—take another road by learning something new. It doesn't have to be an extreme sport or daring endeavor. It just needs to stimulate your brain in new ways. And it needs to be difficult, uncomfortable, awkward—like anything worthwhile you've ever learned. The gold is in the floundering.

We need the chance to fumble, flounder, fall flat on our faces. We need to experience *Beginner's Mind*. As adults, we get so caught up in our egos that we're afraid of being bad at anything. We take ownership in such limiting beliefs as *I'm no good at painting*, or *I have no sense of balance*. How many toddlers say, *I'm no good at walking*, then crawl the rest of their lives? It all comes down to desire. I recently saw a video of a skateboarder with no legs! And he was incredible! Each of us can learn what we want to learn. But we must want it, and we must want it *badly*.

When we're young, we want to do everything. We go through phases where we want to be astronauts, dancers, movie stars, magicians. Our world is an ocean of endless opportunity, our futures as bright as the noonday sun. We can recreate this experience as adults by opening new pathways in the brain. Those opportunities—they're still endless! All that's required is trying something new.

Life loses its meaning when we close ourselves off from the world. When we find proficiency in our chosen skills, we become know-it-alls and life's magic slowly fades. *Learning* puts us back into the dance. What would it be like to see through the eyes of a child? What if you could see everything objectively, without prejudice? What if you opened your mind to the infinite sea of opportunity that surrounds us all?

The fact is... life does not lose its meaning. We do. The world becomes unrecognizable when we refuse to evolve with it. Deeper, we crawl into our caves, blocking out all light except for what streams through a glowing rectangle in the center of the room. We become hypnotized by news, propaganda, biased facts. Our world becomes filled with endless problems because that's all we can see. We forget that all we must do is step outside, feel the sunshine on our face, the wind in our hair, and say:

My God, where have I been?

Look at these arms—they still work!
Look at these legs—they still walk!
Look at this heart—it still beats!
Look at that sun—it still shines!

That's why I love learning new ways to interact with this amazing world. Because throughout all the chaos, I'm able to carve out little slices of meaning. New life rafts on which to navigate, progress, evolve.

After my first successful afternoon of winging, I returned to Valerie with aching arms and tired legs. My stomach grumbled because, through all the excitement, I'd forgotten to eat. Yet before I raided the fridge, I anxiously researched the next day's weather reports and wind speeds. I daydreamed about Hawaii, Malaysia, Argentina and what it might be like to go winging in those places! But then I calmed down and took a deep breath, careful not to get ahead of myself. There's this vast blue ocean just steps from my door. Then I felt a wave of deep, decadent gratitude—for my life, my health, my body, and that somehow, the universe has guided me here, of all possible places, to this moment. Right here. Right now.

That's what it's all about.

As a wise fisherman once explained, it's not the fish he's after. It's the ineffable. That connection to something greater. That feeling that reminds us we're still alive.

Our meaningful activities allow us opportunities to declutter our minds and simply experience life. We become empty vessels—ready to be filled with the divine. We must rekindle our Beginner's Mind, break from our shells, lose our egos, and rejoin the great dance of life. As the rest of the Earthlings dance with style and grace.

People generally suffer from one of two things: a life too short or a life too long. The average human now lives 72 years. That's a long time if we don't evolve throughout its course. Fortunately, there's no law that says you have to be the same person today as you were yesterday.

Change keeps us involved. It keeps us from getting dissociated or depressed. It keeps us alive. When we pursue meaningful activities, we don't have time to be depressed, and we're not searching for artificial stimulants because we're already high. We have our stoke.

Wanting to feel high is natural. When we're continually learning and experiencing new things, we are connected with our natural state of ecstasy. There's enough to carry us through the day. Through our lives. This state of being sharpens our minds, exercises our bodies, keeps our arteries clear. We become vibrant, happy Earthlings.

Are the activities I pursue dangerous? Certainly. But personally, I'd rather be killed in an avalanche or eaten by a shark than die in a hospital bed under fluorescent lighting with clogged arteries after a sedentary life. At least I'll go out with a bang. And it'll be a good story to boot.

Again, it's all about calculated risk. Throwing caution to the wind is a reckless proposition that can easily lead to disaster. Have you seen *Into The Wild*? It's critically important that we take necessary precautions and decrease our risk factors until we deem them *acceptable*. However, you must do the research yourself. Watch the news, and you'd think people get killed by alligators, bears, and sharks all the time. But the truth is, these kinds of deaths are exceedingly rare. They make news reports because they make good stories.

The deadliest animal is the common mosquito, and most deaths occur from heart attacks, cancer, car accidents, and suicide. The media doesn't report these deaths. They don't make good stories.

The problem is we drink the Kool-Aid...

CHAPTER ELEVEN

Kool Aid

The solution to all this misinformation? Do your own research. Most of what you hear on the news is propaganda. It's meant to make you feel a certain way, and often that's an instillation of fear. This keeps us easily manipulated, turning us into a society that refuses to seek truth. It prevents us from seeking new solutions to problems. It causes people to conform and not question certain facts within their group. This is the definition of arrogance.

Ego + ignorance = arrogance.

This creates a culture of robots. Are we headed there now? Have we become people altogether too arrogant or lazy to bother with the truth? We point at certain accepted facts and say, *That's truth!*, forgetting that a scientist can prove just about anything to be true. It all depends on what findings they're commissioned to prove. Scientists are employed by every industry to "scientifically prove" certain facts that support their agendas. Take environmental lawsuits, for example. The first scientist takes the stand proving that dumping toxic chemicals into the ocean is harmful. Then a second scientist takes the stand proving that it's safe. Which is truth? It all depends on the lawyers, the judges, the jury, the potential loopholes and other legal factors. It's different in every case because science is *dynamic* by nature. To call it "truth" is simply lazy, arrogant, or both. We forget that the world was once flat, the Earth was once the center of the solar system, and cigarettes were once safe. The most important tool of the scientist? The wastebasket, said Einstein.

Denial of truth is worse than telling lies. At least the spreader of lies knows they're lies. But we've become so accustomed to believing whatever the "in-group" accepts that we never question their findings, not realizing that little truth actually exists within any "in-group." Real truth typically resides somewhere in the middle. Because we're so politically divided, hardly anyone looks for a *middle* way.

It's time to start questioning again. Questioning is more patriotic than laziness or arrogance. It means you care. Become curious about the world, and there you cultivate your Beginner's Mind. Do this and you'll grow into a wise, compassionate, happy person. Or, continue believing whatever propaganda comes your way, blaming everyone but yourself for the world's problems, and hoping some savior will come along to make it all better.

This is an exciting time to be alive. Many will prosper while others wallow in fear. What will you choose—truth or the hamster wheel? When we question widely accepted beliefs, the world progresses. When we seek to find a better way, our lives improve. It's time to look for new ideas, read new books, be the change we wish to see in the world.

*"In the Beginner's Mind there are many possibilities...
in the expert's there are few."*
—*Shunryo Suzuki*

CHAPTER TWELVE

Kids Only

Off the coast of Shark Key, a maze of backcountry islets unfurls across the shallow flats. There is no destination other than the mangroves themselves, pockets of wild, untamed beauty.

From the kayak launch on the side of the road, we slide our boats into jewel-toned water and enter the enchanted wilderness. The sky feels larger here somehow, colors more vivid, the sea life more intense. We drift through low-lying clouds and occasional fog as we paddle toward the mangroves.

Soon, entrances to small lagoons appear like doorways to new worlds, each enticing further exploration. In the distance, a succession of islands stretches to the horizon. Each a wilderness within a wilderness.

The water is laced with currents, dimpled here and there by schools of tiny baitfish fleeing predators below. They look like rain falling upward. We keep a watchful eye for sea turtles until we see a strange vessel floating up ahead. Paddling closer, we discover a sort of floating treehouse. A crude sign says KIDS ONLY FISH HOUSE. The curious contraption, made mostly of plywood affixed to floating barrels, has a palm-thatched roof for shade and crab traps for stools. I climb aboard so Valerie can snap a few photos of me under the sign (see back cover).

I'll admit to being a Grown-Up Kid. Some might even call me an expert on the subject—hell, I wrote an entire book called *I Don't Want To Grow Up*. My typical day involves waking with the sunrise, having coffee, then writing for a few hours. The rest of my time, I go outside and play. Essentially, I live like a retired person in a young man's body. I don't keep a schedule, I don't keep a watch, I don't even know what day it is.

But I'm working. Seven days a week, fifty-two weeks a year. A regular workaholic, you might say. A cog in the ol' industrial machine. For, if I stop doing these things, I have no writing material. No writing material means no books. No books mean no business.

What I'm doing is not unique. I simply set my sights on goals that have meaning to me. Is the master carpenter who deeply enjoys his work and hasn't taken a holiday in over a year so different? Who works harder?

I'm not trying to impress or gloat. I'm simply suggesting that if we have to work for a living, we might as well streamline the process, reduce the fractions, find the least common denominators. After basic necessities have been met, life is about doing what we enjoy. Is there anything else that matters? Anything else even to discuss?

I see no choice but to seize the day and sound my barbaric yawp! I'm here now, in this body, under these circumstances. To do and act otherwise is blasphemy. To say I'm grateful is an understatement. This is outlandish abundance! Too good to be true? Perhaps. But what if I had set my sights on mansions and Lamborghinis instead? I might then consider my circumstances a dreadful disappointment.

The point is no one can decide what's meaningful to us. That's the beauty of it—we get to decide. If everyone wanted a blue hat, life would be a lot simpler. But then we'd all be walking around in blue hats. How boring is that?

We recognize beauty when something stands out from the ordinary. A colorful bird. A striking sunset. A peculiar melody. Some unidentifiable creature gurgling up from the sea. These strange, beautiful, and enchanting moments stop us in our tracks—they make life worth living, worthy of another generation, another trip around the sun. We must have meaning. Something we aspire to. Something that moves us beyond our own individuality and keeps us engaged with the world. Evolution is vital. Stagnancy is suicide.

When we stop exploring the possibilities of what it means to be human, the world becomes lifeless and dull. Naturally, we then look for artificial stimulants like drugs or electronics for our fulfill-ment—thus losing touch with the real world.

Whether finding a cure for cancer or learning to finger paint, pursuing meaningful activity leads us toward fulfilling lives. This explains why every profession has happy and unhappy people: The lawyer who practices to make a lot of money becomes a slave of his own making. Meanwhile, his colleague who practices for the sheer joys of justice leads a sustainably fulfilling life. Her actions are driven by meaning rather than greed.

Fulfillment needn't come from work. I've hammered at plenty of unfulfilling jobs to pursue other mean-ingful activities. I've worked in retail, sold cars, and waited tables to fund my wilderness trips. I didn't mind these jobs were unfulfilling because they were part of a larger plan. They were merely tasks that needed to be completed—like setting up a tent in a windstorm, tending to blisters on the side of the trail, changing a flat tire on a road trip. With broader perspectives, anything in life can be seen as meaning-ful. As a captain prepares to sail around the world, she must prepare for her voyage with certain duties: repainting the hull, repairing sails, working side jobs to fund her journey to the far side of the world. Contrary to what our social media posts might depict, life is not all sunsets and margaritas. We must put in the work to achieve our dreams.

I'm not saying we need to be world explorers to lead meaningful lives. There just needs to be something beyond the horizon to which we're aspiring and working toward. Some skill or hobby that keeps us connected with the world. Some activity that pushes us to become better, more interested versions of ourselves. It could be refinishing old furniture, collecting antiques, assembling a stamp collection. No activity is too big or too small if it holds deep personal meaning to you.

In any activity, there comes a time when its course has run dry. We can only improve so much until we reach a threshold. A baseball player who relies on constant improvement will eventually fall to despair if he does not find a new passion once his body passes its prime. But the athlete who coaches or telecasts or photographs landscapes finds new peaks to climb, excelling at many lifelong passions. If we set our sights on a single peak, our elation is short-lived when we reach the top, and we find we cannot climb any further. The only way to continue climbing is by setting sights on new peaks. Then it's a steep descent into the dark forests, the lonely valleys, another grueling climb to the top. But the adventure continues.

The show goes on!

Life is not a journey to a mountaintop but a world of endless peaks to explore, rippling as far as the eyes can see beyond the horizon. That's why I'm here by the ocean. I need to keep exploring. When we stop being curious about this mighty big world, we begin to wither away. This explains why retirement is rewarding for some but not for all. It's difficult to find meaning doing nothing. We obsess and scan news headlines for the latest propaganda, ranting about political issues, drifting further and further into delirium. I see this with people who become bitter in old age, speaking of how things used to be in "the good ol' days." Deeper they recede inside their minds, further from the real world, until they no longer recognize it as their own. Connection is lost. Meaning is gone. They become strangers in a strange land. A foreign country that no longer feels like home. Then, they finally check out for good.

Meanwhile, in the house next door, 82-year-old Martha is painting birds outside her window. To her, life is so exciting because there are so many birds she wishes to paint. So many birds, so little time! Enthusiastically she paints away, each brush stroke refining her skills. She consults her guidebooks for their names, researching their migration patterns, anticipating what might grace her window come winter. Each year she plans a trip someplace she's never been, to paint birds she's never seen. News, headlines, politics? She couldn't care less. *The good ol' days?* They're all good days as far as she's concerned. Sure, she has her aches and pains that poke and prod. But who doesn't?

When our lives are filled with this kind of deep meaning, we can enjoy our lives even as conditions grow harsh. Our activities keep us afloat, moving and evolving, progressing forward. With our eyes fixed on a meaningful objective, we can handle any weather. When we lose sight of our dreams, we get lost in the storm.

> *"There are many ways of going forward,*
> *but only one way of standing still."*
> —*Franklin D. Roosevelt*

The idle mind is the devil's workshop. So goes the ancient phrase. Pursuing meaningful activity keeps us out of trouble. With nothing to focus on, the mind is left to fester, latching onto anything that passes by. This often leads to a complete loss of control of our thoughts, a condition that has become disturbingly common in recent times. In a society filled with constant distractions, we are seeing more mental illness than ever before. With so much information coming to us at once, we've become victims to our own devices—buying crap we don't need, worrying about problems beyond our control, angering over trivial concerns. Our emotions have become chaotic. Elated one moment, depressed the next, everything influenced, determined by what's flashing on screens before our eyes. A literal roller coaster of random thoughts.

We think we have individuality, but this is hardly the case. Millions march to the beat of the same drum, thinking the same thoughts, craving the same gadgets, wandering in the same aimless fashions. We set goals we think are unique but prove to be little more than variations of the same theme, always based on what society wants us to crave. Individuality is thrown by the wayside as we become groomed, conditioned, tenderized, desensitized, like cows in line for the slaughterhouse. Anything that goes against the prescribed narrative is censored in today's cancel culture that demonizes ideas that contradict mainstream thought. Thinking outside the box has become all but illegal.

Fortunately, there is a way out of this sheep-like mentality. But it involves curbing our addiction to the most powerful drug of modern times—our electronics. How many of us disconnect for a single hour? A single day? A single week at a time?

Try this. Use those precious vacation days. Those sick days, holidays, personal days. Rent a cabin in the woods or a bungalow by the sea. Or better yet, head to your nearest wilderness (NO SERVICE) and start walking with only a backpack, sleeping bag, perhaps a bag of nuts. Turn off the world for three or four days and listen to that chatter inside your mind. That nonstop reel of chaotic noise that controls your every thought and desire. Watch and observe these strange images—which are not your own and have little to do with who you are.

Watch them from afar, like you're *eavesdropping*, until all that noise seems so bizarre, so abstract, so alien, that you no longer identify with it. Then watch it drift away like leaves on a fall day.

This might take a while, especially if it's been some time since you last disconnected. Days? Weeks? Eventually, you might notice a slight decrease in volume. Or you'll simply lose interest in these incessant thoughts and let them fade into background noise. As the days pass without electronics, watch what changes occur inside your body. Notice how your breathing changes. Your heartbeat, your circulation, your digestive patterns. Pay attention to how you move and how you perform mundane tasks. What else do you notice? Do your mannerisms change? Your sleeping patterns? Your dreams? Write these things down. You'll need them later when you return to the sea of madness. If you could write a letter to your future self, what would it say?

We don't know what we're missing until we step outside the illusion and discover that pristine version of ourselves. The only one that matters.

Everything else is noise.

I've spent decades wandering mountains, oceans, and deserts, searching for a way to bring truth back to the world. But you don't have to walk off into the wilderness to find truth, so long as you find a way to connect with the Earth's natural rhythms in a way that has deep meaning to you.

I've found meaning in activities that involve flowing with gravity, drifting with Mother Nature's currents, channeling her silent messages through a ballpoint pen. Things that involve surfing the forces of nature rather than fighting them. Finding my own unique ways to dance.

When I'm immersed in such activities, I lose the chatter and become hyper-focused on the present moment. During these periods of intense clarity, my mind functions as nature intended. I'm a sane human. Once upon a time, our lives were filled with highly focused attention and impeccable skills necessary for survival. To let the mind wander was to be killed. When times were tough, there was no sitting around collecting unemployment. You swam or you drowned.

We've created the world we live in, and while it has its advantages, life is not as simple as it once was.

To navigate the complexities of modern times, we must become aware of the peculiarity of our predicament. It's not enough to look to those around us— we must step outside this "new normal" and create our own worlds. Otherwise, it creates us, turns us into machines.

"We create our buildings and then they create us. Likewise, we construct our circle of friends and our communities and then they construct us."
—*Franklin Lloyd Wright*

CHAPTER THIRTEEN

The Peace River

Down.
Down.
Down the peaceful Peace River...

The Peace River flows through a wooded area of
central Florida, once home to the Calusa Native
Americans who lived off the land for generations.
As settlers arrived, tensions between the newcomers
and the tribe mounted. Eventually, both sides
agreed to a treaty, using the river as a dividing line

to keep the peace. This worked for a while... until we violated the treaty and destroyed the Native American plantations. It gets worse from here.

Originating at Saddle Creek in Bartow, just east of Tampa, the peaceful Peace River flows 106 miles south to Charlotte Harbor, where it spills into Gasparilla Sound. Our niece is coming to visit for the weekend and wants to go canoeing. It's time to float a river.

We drive north from the Keys to the quaint town of Arcadia. A huge gopher turtle greets us at the mom-and-pop canoe outfitter we stop at to rent our vessels. Inside, the clerk cradles a baby alligator as she collects our money. Outside, we wait beside the river for a shuttle to take us upstream. From there, the plan is to leisurely float back to Arcadia. While it'd be nice to float each of the 106 miles of Peace River, our niece is on a tight schedule with work on Monday. For this adventure, a ten-mile stretch will have to do.

The shuttle picks us up, and drives us into the swampy backwoods of Florida. The trailer carrying our canoes rattles and groans as we watch vultures pick at splayed roadside carcasses. The greatest invention of all time? Roads. At least as far as the vultures are concerned. The jungle thickens the deeper we get. We pass bait shops, shacks, shanties. Life is simple out here in the sticks. Though not as simple as it once was. These shacks and shanties might not have much, but you can bet they get internet. YouTube, Netflix, TikTok, Pornhub—everyone is connected these days, even in the swamps. This saddens me, imagining a time when it was possible to move out to a place like this and be removed from society. When a campfire, a jug of moonshine, and the shooting stars of the Milky Way were the only entertainment required. Satellite TV brought those days to an end. Of course, we could disconnect if we *wanted* to. Yeah right. Rich or poor, young or old, baby boomer or millennial—we all have one thing in common: we're all addicted to the *World Wide Web.*

Down.
Down.
Down the peaceful Peace River...

We pass hunting preserves, airboat outfitters, fish camps, a large dumpster with *Raccoon Café* spray-painted on the side. Then, turning back toward the Peace River, we arrive at our put-in point. The driver helps us organize gear—canoes, paddles, life vests, bag of sandwiches, cooler of beer—then wishes us good luck before skidding away in his short bus, leaving us alone by this lazy river. As the dust settles, we glance at each other, then to the river. Nothing left to do but push off, stay upright, try not to get eaten by gators. We drag our canoes through the sand and set off into the mist.

Birds are everywhere—spoonbills, cranes, terns, the endless circling of vultures. Waiting for us to die.

We pass floating logs, downed trees, uprooted palms. Everything looks like a gator. Drifting silently through the fog, streams of sunlight penetrate the thick canopy overhead, reflecting off the water's surface, blinding our eyes.

Tempting us onshore are pretty white beaches. We stop at one and go exploring. I poke around the muddy bottom and discover a half-buried antique beer can, the old pull-tab style. How this relic hasn't completely eroded in this humid climate baffles me.

Down.
Down.
Down the peaceful Peace River...

Back in the boats, we spy our first gator. An adolescent, about three feet long, hiding in some branches. Quietly, we drift by. He makes not a move. Neither do we.

On stumps and rocks, turtles sun themselves. Spotted catfish dart out from beneath our boats. After a while, we tire of paddling and tie our canoes together with socks. Now we float as a barge— lazy man's way. Interestingly, this helps the canoes track: just a few strokes to the left, a few to the right, is all it takes to keep us pointed steadily downstream. We kick our feet up on the gunwales and crack a beer, enjoying the ride. Conversations flow as we pass more gators, some as long as seven feet. They don't bother us, we don't bother them. A mindset that's worked for generations.

Live and let live. Live and let die?

Either way, we creatures seem to get along best when we live our lives and allow others to live theirs. It's when we try to intervene amongst each other that everything goes to shit. We get too smart for our own good, deeming ourselves *morally superior*. This leads to totalitarianism, genocide, social unrest. History ebbs and flows, rises and falls, repeats itself again and again.

But history is so *yesterday*. It's the media that matters nowadays, right? The truth! Or whatever truths our politically biased, agenda-driven media outlets have deemed factual this week. If there's one thing we can agree on, our side is right and the other is wrong. And we're all 100 percent sure of this. As 100 percent sure as those who say their God is the only God.

We're so full of ourselves. We forget to consider that nature is full of opposing forces—there's a yin to every yang—and neither side is *wrong*. Yet we continue to assert it's our side that matters. The other side should be banned, silenced, censored, exterminated! So we cancel them, boot them from our social groups, ban them from our media outlets. *Second-class citizens!*, we proclaim.

Lock 'em up. Put 'em in camps. Send 'em off to foreign lands. Show me your papers!

It gets worse from here.

Down.
Down.
Down the peaceful Peace River...

CHAPTER FOURTEEN

Riding the Tides

There are two types of people in this world. Those who *force* and those who *adapt*. We know the former too well, as they push and shove their way through life, expecting everyone to change but themselves. They're often rude, demand special attention and burst out if they don't get it. They're also angry, for when you try to force things your way, life is a constant struggle.

Those who *adapt* use existing forces of nature to their own advantage. They ride the tides and surf the rhythms of life. Constantly, they're fine-tuning their preferences until they blend seamlessly with their environment. The world appears to cater to their every need because they are masters of their universe. If they go to a restaurant and don't like the food, instead of a tantrum, they choose a different joint next time. If they run a business, rather than micromanaging and breathing down their employee's necks, they treat them with trust and respect. Carefully they coach each team member to be the best they can be, playing to their own strengths. If a particular employee cannot live up to their company's standards, management politely dismisses them and finds someone else. They eventually surround themselves with highly competent people who require little managing.

In my teens, I waited tables at a pizza joint called LaRosa's. Once a week, the same grumpy old man would plop himself down, place his order, and complain about his food. One day he comes in, sits at his usual table, and I take his order. When I bring out his pizza, he takes a few bites and, with a scowl, demands to see the manager. I bring my manager out, and the old man just goes off. "The crust, the bacon, the sauce, everything is wrong!"

he snarls. Then, looking directly into my manager's eyes, he growls, "Every time I come here, you screw up my pizza!" When the old man's rants subside, my manager looks at him calmly. "Sir," he says, "if every time you come here, we screw up your pizza, why do you keep coming?"

The adaptive person would have found another pizza place long ago, saving everyone a lot of time and aggravation. But this man just kept coming back, hoping it would somehow change. Or perhaps he was holding on to some idea of what it once was years ago. We figured at some point he *must* have liked the pizza? Constantly trying to force the world to cater to our selfish needs makes us destined to become like the grumpy old man.

The same is true with artists. The difference between a good painter and an exceptional painter is his ability to adapt. When starting a piece, he might have in mind the image of a cat. If he's not adaptable, he may quickly become frustrated when the painting isn't working the way he'd planned. The exceptional painter is adaptable. He may begin with the image of a cat, only to find out halfway through that it's a mountain, a sunrise, or a beautiful girl.

"If you want to make God laugh,
tell him about your plans."
—*Woody Allen*

Likewise, an author who forces his characters into action is rarely believable. The exceptional author never forces. He listens—remembering that he's simply the messenger. He allows the story to tell itself, going whichever way it pleases. He lets his characters come alive and doesn't usually know where things are going until he writes them down. When a surprising twist occurs in the plot, the exceptional writer is surprised as we. That's what makes great novels *great*. We go on and on about who is a great writer when they're actually a great listener.

When we try to control narratives, we become immune to new information. When we allow truths to surface naturally, we open ourselves to new possibilities—solutions to problems come easily and rapidly.

Such a way of living was considered common sense in generations past. You couldn't force your crops to grow or a storm to retreat. Those who refused to adapt did not survive.

When I'm backpacking through the mountains, I cannot force my way across a raging river. I must find a way around, sometimes walking miles in the *wrong direction* until I discover a safe crossing. Likewise, when I'm wing foiling, I cannot force the wind to blow in the direction I want to go. I must work with nature by adjusting my sail and slowly tacking upwind. As rudimentary as this might seem, this simple wisdom is going by the wayside because we've confined ourselves to digital realities and industrialized landscapes.

Humans have an uncanny knack for bulldozing through nature, like spoiled children wrecking their toys. Give us a forest and we'll log it, give us a mountain and we'll mine it, give us an ocean and we'll pollute it. We do these things to make our lives better, we reason. Engineered pleasures and electronic vistas are safer, more accessible, *and* more profitable, we insist. And they're available to everyone! This attitude has catalyzed the ecological catastrophe we now face.

Many of today's jobs have us repeating the same tasks day after day. Essentially, we get paid to put up with monotony. This may have been tolerable when workdays ended at 5 p.m., but now the true nine-to-five has become a thing of the past. My father worked full-time to raise our family, but he was home by suppertime to take us fishing, toss the baseball, or help us build tree forts. Now our jobs keep us working late into the evenings, overflowing into our precious weekends. We have vacation days but are made to feel guilty using them with tight schedules and looming deadlines.

We do all of this for the sake of *security*. Yet security cannot be found in an ever-changing world. Economies collapse, jobs disappear, industries change. This is happening faster every day. This so-called security we're desperately chasing—it is an illusion, a phantom, a ghost. Life changes and we must evolve with it. There's only one way to survive this rapidly changing world: We must learn to ride the tides.

CHAPTER FIFTEEN

Days on The Wing

I suppose I'm trying to live more like an animal. We *Homo sapiens* were once highly skilled creatures—climbing trees, escaping predators, chasing prey. Only recently have we replaced these rudimentary tasks with computer skills and the like. We now can navigate computers and smartphones with grace yet blunder through our natural habitats like buffoons.

When I sit on the beach and watch the gulls, not a single bird misses a beat. They are master flyers and fishermen, plummeting into the sea to catch a fish, then soaring on motionless wings, rising and falling with rhythmic beauty. They never seem bored because they do not subject themselves to cubicles, nor do they impose silly rules about how they must fly. This is not to say I wish to be a gull, I'm simply enamored with their profound sense of style and grace. If I can achieve similar levels as a human, how could I resist?

Lately, I've been living according to the wind. Waking, fixing coffee, checking weather reports. If the wind comes in the morning, I go foiling and then write in the afternoon. If windy in the afternoon, I flip my schedule. I love this feeling, continually excited for what each day might bring. My world becomes immersed in the rhythms of tide charts, winds speeds, wave reports—eager to predict what gifts Mother Nature might leave under the tree.

Optimal experience. That's what I'm after. To connect with my primal nature, to be fully engaged. Meaningful activity as an end in itself. No benefits except the promise of proficiency. I'm addicted, to be sure. But each day, Mother Nature teaches me new things. It's a lifelong lesson—slowly I'm learning what it means to be an Earthling.

Initially, wing foiling was all about balance and control. How to stand on the board, hold the wing, not get knocked over by waves. As I've progressed, these fundamentals have become automatic. Now it's all about learning the rhythms of the sea—how to read her swells and ride her waves, making it effortless as possible. I'm learning to ride the valleys between the waves, building momentum as the next swell surges behind. When I feel the power of the wave approaching, I release my grip on the wing and let it flag behind me. Now I'm surfing. When the wave ends, I reposition my wing perpendicular to the wind, racing back out to catch another. All the while, I'm observing the wildlife pulsing around me. Osprey, eagles, spoonbills. Dolphins, manatees, rays. It's mating season and copulating sea turtles are everywhere. At night they crawl onto the beach to bury their eggs, and in the morning, you see their tracks. Local conservation efforts rope off these areas, protecting their eggs from children who love nothing more than to dig in the sand.

Standing on my board, my head is eight feet above the water. From this vantage, I can easily observe the stream of creatures passing so languidly below.

Occasionally something unidentifiable lunges for my hydrofoil—from underwater I must look like a stingray. Adrenaline courses through my body.

Don't crash now!

My heart skips a beat. My muscles tighten. A wave of fear comes over me, but it's not enough to wash the smile off my face. The whole time I operate in a state of complete disbelief—that this kind of human experience is possible. That this much fun exists! This technology exists! It's utterly ridiculous.

Sometimes I lean back like I'm reclining in an invisible chair. The wind-powered wing supports my arms, gravity pulls at my feet, and I relax into a feeling of weightlessness. When the winds are steady, I can maintain this posture for several minutes. These little "breaks" are much needed as it takes a lot of energy to get out past the shore break. Wading through the surf, my foil board in one hand and my wing in the other can be a lot to manage. Any misjudgment could send me tumbling, possibly damaging my equipment, which is expensive, or my body, which is more expensive. Complete immersion in the present moment is crucial. Any lapse in attention can lead to disaster.

Luckily, I've been fortunate in my endeavors. A single broken bone in 47 years of my thrill-seeking lifestyle—skateboarding, of course. But I've had plenty of scrapes, scabs, cuts, bruises, twists, sprains, and other ailments that have sent me limping, sleeping on one side, or going to the emergency room for stitches. I've got the scars to prove it.

"Fun marks," I call them.

But that's life. I like to look at life not in terms of years but by the number of smiles. Would I like to live to the ripe old age of 95? Sure, but longevity is far from the point. How many smiles can I have today? That's what I'm after. What happens tomorrow is out of my control.

"Wrinkles only go where the smiles have been."
—Jimmy Buffett

Why attempt to control that which we cannot control? Sounds like a good way to end up in the loony bin. Life is a sea of moments, a constant stream of nows, and then you die. The only thing you can control is *this* now—the only one that exists.

What puts a smile on your face? *Now* do that. Keep doing that until you're no longer smiling. *Now* do something else.

Repeat as necessary.

Most of us can't live this way because we're invested in future *nows*. This is putting all your eggs in one basket. Future *nows* are highly speculative investments because there's no guarantee they'll ever come. To exacerbate things further, when tomorrow's *now* finally arrives, we shift focus to another future *now*.

When do we ever get to this elusive future *now* that we spend our entire lives preparing for? That's right, tomorrow...

> *"FREE BEER TOMORROW"*
> —*Sign at local bar*

Lately, the wind has been arriving in the afternoons, leaving my days free to write my newest book, the one you're reading now: *Oceans Of My Mind*. Valerie recently pointed out that its initials spell

Oomm, the drawn-out pronunciation of the sacred symbol *Om*, representing consciousness. This seems appropriate, as I feel my mind becoming formless, shapeless, malleable like the sea. I'm beginning to flow like water. Learning this delicate art of dancing on the sea. Of course, you don't really dance *on* it. You dance *with* it.

This connection is my religion, merging with wind, water, waves, the Great Happening. With God herself. In these sacred moments, my ego dissolves. No more Scott Stillman, no more author—just the blazing fire of *now*.

I'm reminded of my true identity. Grateful in this human body yet humbled by its impermanence. For my flesh is fleeting like a wave, but I am eternal like the sea. In this revelation, I realize that I *can* surf that eternal wave because each time a wave dies, another is born. They just keep coming.

The rhythm never stops.

There's so much beauty I want to experience. My biggest fear in life is dying before I get to see it all. But when I'm sailing across the open ocean, my fear disappears and I simply relax into enjoying what's happening now. Because *now* is all there ever is to see.

The powerboats have all but disappeared and it's just me and the sea life. Tarpon are migrating by the thousands, swimming north along the coast in a constant stream from morning until night. Many stretch six feet long, their schools so thick I repeatedly bump into them while foiling. I'm convinced this doesn't harm them—the leading edge of my hydrofoil is rounded and fish dart quickly away.

The abundance of wildlife seems to be increasing with the turn of the season, not just below the water but also on land. Turtles, rabbits, lizards galore. Frogs and toads are everywhere, some the size of my hand, others the size of my fingernail. There are alligators in the swamps, iguanas in the trees, and tiny deer called Key Deer which live nowhere else but the Keys. Crabs work the grave shift, prowling the grounds in a curious array of shapes, sizes, and colorations. Birds clamor to the point we've begun closing our windows at night to sleep.

Days become rituals, organizing gear, transporting everything to the beach, unpacking the wing, attaching the hydrofoil, making sure everything is properly secured before casting off for adventure. Slowly, methodically, breathing into each task. Owning it. The mind does not wander.

In the evenings, I'm happily exhausted. Content with a hot shower, a cold beer, a relaxing evening cuddling with Valerie on the veranda. There's no anxiousness, no craving. No longing to be anywhere but here.

I wonder if similar levels of satisfaction are attainable as a tradesman of sorts, someone who engages with work involving specialized skills, physical labor, an ever-changing landscape of new challenges to overcome. Anything that pushes the limits of mind, body, and soul.

It's when I simply go through the motions I get into trouble. That's when the longing creeps in. The restlessness. The desire to be somewhere else. We often stay in these unfulfilling roles far too long, wasting months, years, decades of our lives chasing that dangling carrot of future comforts.

"The lust for comfort
murders the passion of the soul."
—*Khalil Gibran*

CHAPTER SIXTEEN

Geiger Key

A group of low-flying pelicans casts their reflection across the flats extending out to sea. We launch into a large bay known as Similar Sound. Beneath our hulls, sea sponges texture the ocean floor; we paddle over them toward this morning's destination— a group of coral heads a few miles out into the open ocean.

To be alone, this is the place. It's far enough away from the highway you can't hear the traffic, the water is too skinny for motorboats, and there are enough tiny islets and coves to provide each explorer their own solitude for days. The views out to sea go on forever, liberating the mind, pacifying the soul.

Along the way, we explore Saddlebunch Key, Bird Key, and a few unnamed others. Each is an invitation for us to visit their secret worlds, supporting great populations of clamoring seabirds. Songs vary within each community, from simple and melodic, to gay as playground noise, to somber as love songs. When we venture too closely to their nests, we're scolded by the wild and threatening cries of eagles and ospreys guarding their young. As always, the swarms of gulls hang above our heads, flying in psychic unity, scattering, diving, rising and falling to some kind of instinctual language. Thinking as one, moving as one, like the shoals of fish beneath our hulls.

It's all so damn beautiful—the ocean, the beaches, the islands, the sea life. The longer we stay here, the deeper our admiration becomes and the more we wish to know. It's amazing, really, that despite the odds, we've somehow managed not to spoil these places completely. It's a privilege to come to know these different worlds. To step outside our computerized, air-conditioned, jet-propelled lives and concern ourselves with the worlds of birds, fish, corals. To feel that nature is still intact, that her rhythms still go on. Without nature, there is no humanity. She's my sole connection to God. Her daily sermons remind me that we're included in something much larger than our self-serving aspirations. With or without us, there is no pause in the singing of birds, the blowing of winds, the breaking of waves, the ebbing and flowing of tides.

Leaving the mangroves, we head toward the open sea. A fierce headwind slows our progress, but with the warm water splashing atop the kayaks, we feel energized. We paddle hard until reaching a patch of blue where the coral heads are reported to be. Our guidebook enticed us with colorful photos of blue angelfish, striped parrotfish, spotted eagle rays, hawksbill turtles. Valerie and I jump in with masks and snorkels but find only seaweed and sand—the reefs are nowhere to be seen. Rather than abort the mission entirely, we decide to stay in the water, drifting back toward the mangroves with the wind, our vessels tethered to our ankles, never trailing too far behind.

Though we'd hoped to find the coral heads, what we stumble upon instead is a privilege to behold. Flurries of stingrays flee their hiding places in great puffs of sand, moving stealthily along the ocean floor with the flaps of their muscular wings. Such simple ecstasy, swimming among these great birds of the sea, suspended between two worlds. Stingrays will use their stingers only as a last resort, preferring to avoid danger rather than confront it.

We pass spiny lobsters, horseshoe crabs, urchins, starfish, moon jellies, sea anemones. Much like the desert, everything on the ocean floor tends to sting, stab, stick, or prick. Life is best observed rather than touched. We get along best when we don't interfere.

Sunlight beams and bends through the water, illuminating swaying meadows of shoal grass, manatee grass, and ribbon-like turtle grass that brush against our bellies while we drift through the shallows. Much like land grasses use wind for pollination, seagrasses use the movements of water to carry their cells and reproduce. These underwater forests form unique habitats, providing food and shelter for many species of fish and wildlife. In recent years, they've become threatened by coastal construction, dredging, powerboating, and fertilizer run-off. Shallow, easily polluted waters like these are essential to the survival of sealife.

With nowhere to stand, we keep floating with our masks and snorkels until we reach the mangroves. There, a deep underwater chasm bustling with thousands of tropical fish awaits us. I dive down deep, searching for parrotfish hiding in underwater caves, under ledges, among the twisted mangrove roots, experiencing the peculiar feeling of being underground. Angled sunlight penetrates the far reaches of the chasm, revealing colorful drums, grunts, porkfish. A moray eel flashes in the light, electrical jellyfish appear illuminated from within. A kaleidoscope of imagery dances and flickers before our eyes.

We resurface and climb back into our boats, paddling back to Geiger Key, happy, exhausted. Ready for cold beers and fish sandwiches.

CHAPTER SEVENTEEN

Saving The Human Race

Why do people sail the seven seas, climb the highest peaks, surf the largest waves? Some dedicate their lives to these pursuits, surviving on shoestring budgets, living in cars, risking their lives for the thrill of adventure. What's the motivation behind these seemingly frivolous endeavors? What is the point?

To attempt an answer, we must ask another question: What is the point of life?

To this question, we get different responses. The most popular answer is obvious: to raise a family. While procreation is the primary goal of any species, if we take all our human problems and boil them down to one underlying issue, the answer is strikingly obvious: overpopulation. It's at the core of air pollution, water pollution, deforestation, over-fishing, over-grazing, over-everything. When there were fewer people in this world, we could exploit our natural resources with wild abandon. With our current overpopulation issue, however, no matter how you slice it, we're fighting a losing battle. The Earth simply cannot sustain eight billion humans.

Why then, do so many dedicate their lives to procreation? What is this insatiable urge to reproduce at such an alarming rate when our species is already at the brink of collapse? Take a look around— for the first time in history, human extinction is actually within striking distance!

This threat is not to Mother Nature. She can take care of herself, as she's done long since before we arrived. The threat is to humanity itself. We'll control overpopulation, or Mother Nature will course-correct with things like viruses, tsunamis, earthquakes, infertility.

Why is infertility on the rise? Why are we increasingly more attracted to same sex partners? Why can't we read the writing on the wall? Mother Nature is adapting to rapidly changing conditions—and this is good! It's how she survives.

My point here is not to argue whether you should procreate. My point is in today's overpopulated world, procreating is no less frivolous than climbing the world's highest peaks, surfing the biggest waves, or assembling the world's largest stamp collection. The fact is society *wants* you to procreate. More humans equal more business. More mouths to feed, more clothes to manufacture, more gadgets, computers, cellphones, insurance policies, furniture, bank accounts, car dealerships, housing developments. Procreation keeps the economy in check. Surfing, sailing, and climbing mountains do not.

These ideas may seem obscure yet look to nature and you will see otherwise. Animals reproduce, but they don't dedicate their entire lives to the pursuit. While not procuring food or making babies, our scaled, feathered, and furry friends spend most of their time playing and enjoying themselves. Birds spend much of their time just flying around. Squirrels and chipmunks are regular Evel Knievels, making death-defying leaps, skipping across telephone wires, racing across busy highways. They sometimes get squashed, yet they don't seem to make too much of a fuss about it. When is the last time you saw a congregation of squirrels gathered around their smashed cousin on the side of the road, gathering up remains for a proper burial? They just get squashed, then picked over by turkey vultures, then eaten by worms. Their bodies decompose as nature intended. These animals don't *want* to die, but they seem to accept it as a natural part of life. Humans, on the other hand, are petrified of this natural occurrence. Hastily we cover up death, hiding our remains in bronze caskets topped with expensive bouquets of flowers.

Seven thousand people die per day in America. That's a lot of funerals. Death is quite the industry itself, and we spend a lot of money covering it up. Does this help or hinder our unhealthy fear of annihilation? We don't cover up birth. Why death? Is dying less natural than being born? When someone dies surfing a giant wave in Australia, is it a tragedy? Any more or less so than raising a family and dying of heart disease at 72?

I wish neither to compare nor judge lifestyle choices. I simply wish to make a case for the dirt-bag, the ski bum, the surf junkie, the river rat. All reasonable, responsible, noble life pursuits.

Many of us crave a simpler life, yet preconceived ideas and molded comforts aim to keep us on the righteous beaten path. Teachers persuade children to do something with their lives and *contribute* to the world. Yet, in today's overpopulated, over-industrialized world, one could easily argue the best, most meaningful contribution they could make is to *not contribute*. To leave the smallest footprint possible. Is this not sustainability? Is this not evolution?

I'm not saying we should all quit our jobs and become surf bums or stop raising families and leave our deceased lying dead in the streets. I'm simply wondering if we shouldn't re-examine what we call *meaningful activity*—what it actually means to be humans? What's possible outside of life as a data analyst, a computer programmer, a software engineer? Do we really need another iPhone? Or do we need to get back to the basics of what it means to be Earthlings?

We are seeing changes today far beyond anything our ancestors could've imagined. We order goods and services from computers rather than brick and mortar stores; jobs are being relocated to our homes; long-standing businesses are closing their doors overnight; entire industries are becoming obsolete. Working for one company for thirty years and then retiring on a pension has become a thing of the past. To say the future is uncertain is an understatement. We have spiraled headfirst into a new reality! What will the future hold? How can we learn from the past, what can we project forward? If we are to keep procreating, what kind of world will we create for our children?

I have no answers, only food for thought. That's what these books are about: to critique the society in which we live; to poke and prod at widely accepted beliefs; to expose blind conformity, shatter collective illusions, and dispel the destructive us-versus-them thinking that plagues our society. Books are the final frontier, where independent authors may speak freely from the oceans of our minds, without agenda, nor self-censorship to please certain groups. Can we expect this from CNN, Fox News, commissioned scientists, the government?

*"If the independent author
will not speak truth for us, who will?"*
—Edward Abbey

As I sit here on our veranda this foggy morning overlooking the sea, birds are singing their morning songs, chipmunks are scurrying up tree trunks, lizards are chasing each other along the sea wall, dolphins are playing in the shallows. Oblivious to the world's problems? Perhaps. Irresponsible, reckless, self-serving? Are their pursuits more frivolous than ours? What might they consider meaningful activity? What might we learn from *them*?

The fog thickens, obscuring the horizon with silvery light. A light rain falls, dimpling the surface of the bay. An owl hoots in the trees, hunting for breakfast. Throughout the madness of our human-dominated world, nature perseveres. Living for the sake of living. Something that worked long before our species arrived and will continue long after we are gone.

Humans have been around for approximately 300,000 years, civilization for 6,000 years, and industrialization just 200 years. That's three lifespans. One hundred and thirty-five years ago there were no cars. What types of vessels will we see in the next hundred? Will anyone be around?

The answers lie in a total rethinking of how we live. A complete re-examination of what we consider meaningful activity. A new definition of what it means to be Earthlings.

What is the ultimate goal? To live the longest? To make the most money? To design the next gadget or social media platform, the best self-driving car or airplane or semi-truck or bus?

What then?

What do humans have to offer? Are we worth saving? We strive to save the manatee, the sea turtle, the snow leopard, the spotted owl. How about the human? This strange species that reproduces with wild abandon and destroys everything in its path? Are we noble creatures or an invasive species? What purpose do we serve?

What would stop Mother Nature from pulling the plug?

I think humanity *is* worth saving, but not in its current condition. Our model is beyond unsustainable, doomed to extinction, destined to fail.

Ask a mathematician, a data scientist, a philosopher, anyone with the capacity to look beyond their own lifespan. It's inevitable we're headed for collapse. Economical, ecological, psychological...

A change is gonna come!

Fortunately, the best solutions are often the simplest. How can we get back to meaningful activity? Do we really need another electric vegetable slicer, or should we learn how to use a knife? Do we need an electric bicycle, or should we get ourselves into shape? Do we need a self-driving car, or should we drive less and play more? Do we need a better smartphone, or should we open our eyes to *reality*? The miracle we were born into. The ecstasy that is everyday life.

CHAPTER EIGHTEEN

Navigation

On a picture-perfect December morning, I launch my paddleboard into open waters and skate across the mirror image of a cloudless sky. Gliding effortlessly through the shallows, I gaze over hundreds of sand dollars scattered across the ocean floor. Three dolphins splash about, a mother and her young, playing in the dazzling sunlight. My mind is relaxed and alert as I scan the horizon for perturbations of any kind. One of the great joys of being out on the ocean is the monotony, combined with an underlying level of excitement for what might surface at any moment. I try to imagine what it'd be like to paddle amongst humpback whales, to see a forty-ton creature breaching the surface must be electrifying! But I'm happy enough to be here, and settle into the present of what's before me.

Today, I am heading for the Point Of Rocks— a stretch of coral, rock, and shallow waters where myriad sea creatures love to hide. The place can be violent at high tide, especially with an incoming swell, but when waters are low and calm, it becomes a tranquil area for investigating tide pools and small lagoons. Thousands of shells wash in daily. A person could collect bucketfuls every day and each morning they would be replenished.

When I arrive, schools of snook are patrolling the turquoise-green waters. Crabs sun themselves on exposed rocks. Seabirds fish the shoreline. I park my paddleboard on a stone and walk barefoot across the rocky expanse. Lichens and moss grow on the rocks, they change colors throughout the seasons. Today they glow in vibrant, deep shades of lavender, burnt orange, neon green. Water flows freely over the rocks, swaying the moss back and forth under an inch of seawater, washing in and out with the ocean's rhythms. They are a joy to walk upon barefoot, like a bed of shaggy carpet. The rocks stretch far and wide, providing endless exploration without the need to step on sharp shells. Here and there, gaps in the stone reveal themselves, deep holes swirling and boiling like whirlpools. These contain hundreds of shells, most alive with mollusks and hermit crabs. When the mollusks die, the hermits move in, occupying their empty shells, carrying them along on their backs wherever they go. They cling to the rocks with jointed legs, preventing the surf from washing them away.

The first time I collected shells here, I was alarmed when I'd set them on the kitchen counter to dry, and they started roaming about. I brought back the live ones to the reef, keeping only the unoccupied specimens. Though my inner child wanted to keep the hermits as pets, I knew they'd be much happier back at the reefs. I'll kill to eat, but never for souvenir.

Shoals of fish move in tight bunches, swimming with unanimous precision. When a single fish turns, the rest move simultaneously, avoiding predators and obstacles.

There are two ways to navigate. Focusing on obstacles and focusing on the path. If you're caught in an ocean rip current, trying to out-swim it is a good way to drown. But if you swim with it, conserving energy until the current ceases, you can make it safely to shore. Likewise, if I'm barreling down a winding trail on my mountain bike, if I focus on the trees, I'll crash into them. But if I keep my eyes squarely focused on the path, I can make it safely down the trail. I keep the obstacles in my peripheral vision but never focus on them *directly*. That's a recipe for disaster. I've integrated this crucial lesson into the rest of my life.

Think of rainwater flowing down a sidewalk during a thunderstorm. As it travels, it branches out into different directions, following the many paths of least resistance. In every situation, there are paths of least resistance. The key is cultivating our sense of navigation so we flow effortlessly along these paths without hesitation. We must become like water.

Buddhists call this *getting out of our own way.* When we connect deeply with our environment, we no longer feel separate from the world that surrounds us. This is where transformation occurs. We see the world and all its forces as extensions of ourselves. No longer are we strangers in a strange land but integral parts of a greater force. We develop a second nature similar to a sailor navigating a ship during a storm. Life becomes about honing our skills, an endeavor that keeps us engrossed in the world. Whether flying a plane, sailing a ship, or knitting a wool blanket—it's all about navigation.

This is what separates the fulfilled and the unfulfilled. There must be something we're working toward. Some navigation. Otherwise, we become stagnant. When water gets stagnant, it becomes polluted. Eventually, it dries up completely. We are not so different. Emotionally distressed people often admit feeling paralyzed. At some point, they stopped moving, or they focused on too many obstacles and lost sight of the path. Or perhaps they reached their destination and never set a new one. Successful people often admit that the worst part of having an ambitious goal is achieving it. When our sights are fixed on a meaningful objective, our trajectory is clear. When we reach it, we must have a new destination awaiting. Another voyage, another climb. Or we become aimless wanderers.

Always there must be a point on the horizon, just out of reach, that we are navigating *toward*.

> *"The time to prepare for your next expedition is when you have just returned from a successful trip."*
> —*Robert Peary*

Everything in nature has direction. Plants grow toward the sun. Bees seek the nectar of flowers. Salmon swim upriver to spawn. This keeps the universe functioning as designed. When we have direction, we become part of this harmonious dance, and nature naturally helps guide us toward our goals.

Often my destination is not a specific location but a level of proficiency or understanding. These destinations can be incredibly rewarding as no fixed points exist on a map, yet the journey is real. This kind of journey is common among those recovering from some trauma. Learning to walk after a bad accident, loving after a failed relationship, trusting after betrayal. Tragedy can sometimes lead to life-changing redemption when it gives us direction where we had none before.

Fortunately, you don't have to get in a bad car accident to have direction. Just choose a destination and move toward it. This puts you back in the dance. Your destination can be anything, so long as it has personal meaning to you. Basing your sights on someone else's summit stales the journey, as you live their dream, not your own.

CHAPTER NINETEEN

Rhythm

There's a reason people want to live by the sea. Inland, it's all strip malls and Walmarts. "You can get a house three times the size if you go inland," insists a tourist at our local pub. He's got a point: oceanfront properties do come at a premium. But when I leave the coast, I get anxious. I'll take a shanty by the sea over a landlocked mansion any day. There's just something about hearing the surf, smelling the salty air, walking to the beach without driving a car. I've never made much money in this wacky writing profession, but I've always found a way to live at nature's doorstep. I suppose if you want something badly enough, you *find a way*.

The good thing about knowing precisely what you want is your choices become limited. This laser focus uncovers opportunities that others cannot see. In Captain Liz Clark's inspiring memoir, *Swell*, the author explains her insatiable desire to sail around the world. Only there's two major obstacles:

1. She doesn't own a sailboat.
2. She has no money.

Rather than abandoning her life's purpose, she embeds herself in the sailing community by taking a waitressing job on a mega yacht near Santa Barbara, California. While filling champagne flutes, she meets college professor Dr. Barry Schuyler, who reveals his own once-upon-a-dream of sailing round the world— only his life's responsibilities had gotten in the way and he never went. Now almost eighty years old, he explains his new desire to live vicariously through someone else's sailing adventure... on *his* sailboat! Long story short, she completes her voyage. Now more than 10 years and 20,000 miles later, she's still out there sailing the great seas, living the life of her dreams.

There are two types of people in this world. Those who say, "I can't" and those who say, "How can I?" This simple shift of words changes everything. One closes a door, the other opens it. You can change a dead-end into a gateway simply by adjusting your perspective. When we shift our perspective, anything becomes possible.

Those who point fingers at the rich and privileged, blaming them for their own personal shortcomings, hurt only themselves. Many think money will solve their problems, but it doesn't. Out-of-the-box thinking solves problems. This may *lead* to money, but the thinking comes first, not the other way around.

The problem is that most people go along with the in-crowd. They do what everyone else does. They're afraid of being different, afraid of being ostracized, and they never question widely accepted narratives and popular beliefs.

Nature teaches us to look where others don't. It shows us magic beyond all the strip malls and Walmarts.

When I'm out in the ocean, it seems the sky is the limit and I can do no wrong. Back on shore, my doubts creep back in, but this constant rhythm of coming and going keeps my mind limber. It keeps me refreshed. It keeps me dreaming.

It pains me that not everyone has access to nature this way. This is the missing link. We need connection with nature like we need air to breathe. Otherwise, we become suffocated by whatever narrative surrounds us. I can't live my own story while surrounded by everyone else's. So I go to the wilderness and come back—go away, come back, go away, come back.

> *"I go to the mountains to find myself."*
> *—John Muir*

We become what we feed our minds. Focus on the narrow scope of your world, and your mind becomes narrow. Focus on the vastness of nature's mountains, deserts, and oceans, and your mind becomes vast. In this vastness, everything is possible, for nature knows no wealth, no privilege, no status. Nature is pure potential. If we can learn to tap into this unlimited potential, we see beyond our limiting beliefs.

The movers and shakers of life have all tapped into this place of unlimited potential. They're able to see gateways where others see dead ends. Great art, great jazz, great ideas—they all come from this place of pure potential. You don't have to be smart to be a genius. You just need to tune in to the Earth's wisdom. Unfortunately, it's becoming difficult to hear in our noisy world. To listen clearly, we must welcome nature back into our lives.

> *"I think 99 times and find nothing.*
> *I stop thinking, swim in silence,*
> *and the truth comes to me."*
> —*Albert Einstein*

There's something exciting about the fog. The way it casts its eerie spell, obscuring the landscape with mystery. Trees disappear and all I can see is this great white ball of sun over iridescent water. My immediate surroundings, however, remain in focus. From my paddleboard I see clearly to the ocean floor, connecting me to the sea in an intimate way.

The ocean teems with fish. Sheepshead, mullet, snook, baitfish by the billions. Slowly I creep through the water as they scatter beneath my hull. Colorful reefs in shades of green, orange, and bronze pass below as I drift over sharp corals mere inches from my board. In these shallow zones, where catching my board's fin could unexpectedly crash me onto the reefs, I stagger my stance, allowing me the ability to shift from side to side, forward and backward as needed. I'll fall onto my board if necessary, as crashing into the coral simply isn't an option. These small adjustments become fine-tuned with each outing. For open-ocean cruising, I'm relaxed with feet hip-width apart. For waves, it's surf stance, one foot in front of the other. Proficiency is my goal. To be comfortable in all conditions, all kinds of weather. With proficiency comes deep awareness, deeper cultivation of my relationship with Mother Ocean. We are beginning to understand each other.

In any relationship, there is give and take. Forget this and you'll get eaten alive. Respect nature's rhythms, and a lifetime love affair ensues. Fight her, and life becomes a constant battle.

We are here, not as aliens, but as integral parts of the Earth. Yet, removed as we've become, our once-deep relationship with Mother Nature has grown shallow with neglect and forgotten rituals. We can rekindle our connection by engaging with her elements and surfing her rhythms, preferably under our own power.

Everything can be thought of as a force coming at us. It's our choice to either fight or befriend those forces. If we fight them, we make enemies with Mother Nature. When we befriend them, a deep relationship ensues—with life itself.

What could be better than that?

With this deep bond with Mother Nature, we shall never be lonely, never be without love or support. For if the entire world should crumble, we'd simply befriend the crumbling.

Everything that happens to us, happens *for* us. Though, at first glance, this might be difficult to see, the forces of nature exist for our own benefit. They exist in perfect form, and we are part of this divine perfection. The world is not something to conquer. We must learn to go with its flow. When we learn to navigate life this way, we settle into our own skin, feel the divine perfection of our human bodies, and move through the world with the same style and grace as all other Earthlings.

A skilled sailor tacks slowly upwind until the gales shift in her favor. Then she seizes the opportunity to fly. We can fly too, but sometimes we must tack until things shift in our favor. If the winds never change, we may need to change course altogether. The key is to remain fluid, making subtle adjustments along the way.

Many have so insulated themselves from nature's rhythms that they've lost all touch with their earthly skills. Mental illness creeps in when entire civilizations lose grasp of these basic fundamentals. With the loss of our primitive human traits comes a desperate clinging to security. This is the worst of conditions because security is impossible in an organically changing world. The more we realize our attempts at security are futile, the more we try to force the world to change. Thus, the path of self-destruction ensues. The cycle continues.

It's easy to see this happening today, as it seems our problems have become everyone's but our own.

This constant finger-pointing and blaming causes us to put up barriers as we push and shove our way through the world, fighting whomever and whatever gets in our way. We make enemies with life. The only possible outcome is annihilation. We've seen it all before.

Liberty is all we have. Security is pie in the sky. It's a fugazi—it does not exist. And it isn't worth the price of our freedoms. When we lose the ability to move through life in the direction of our own choosing, liberty is doomed.

> *"He who gives up liberty for security*
> *deserves neither liberty nor security."*
> —*Benjamin Franklin*

Our lives are pulses in an eternal rhythm. We come and go like ocean waves. While you read these words, thousands of people are being born as thousands are dying. The Earth produces humans like it grows oranges and tomatoes. Death and birth are part of the process—all part of a great rhythm that started with the beginning of time and never stops. We are not separate from this. We are the rhythm. Our lives are tiny sparks of observation—and this is entirely the point! We needn't fear death because these sparks go on indefinitely, a pulsing electricity that never ceases to exist. From this perspective, it's easy to see we are part of a greater process. To fear death would be like holding a funeral for an ocean wave. Waves are part of the rhythm.

And the rhythm goes on!

Do you cry each time you eat a banana? Of course not. The banana is a repeatable act and so are you. Next time you might have red hair or dark skin, or you might be covered in fur, scales, or feathers. What an exciting proposition! How boring might it be to live forever? Yet we're so obsessed with safety and security, we'll strap loved ones to hospital beds and cram feeding tubes down their throats just to keep them alive. What is this strange fixation with trying to *stop* the rhythm? What's next? Engineering some sort of sanitized container we can survive in forever? Dining on sterilized food, breathing disinfected air, never driving a car, never drinking an alcoholic beverage, never leaving the security of our safety box? Is this what we so desire—a prison of our own creation? If so, why bother with the whole charade? Seems like an awful lot of work for...

What exactly?

Call me crazy, but I'd rather float down a river pure and free, with only the eagles and buzzards overhead. In this river of life that flows, what is this desperation to cling to the shore? Clinging is hard. Letting go is easy. Why not enjoy the ride? The sooner we do, the sooner we fall back into congruence with life's rhythms, the never-ending dance, those sparks of observation that are our very birthright.

You can't stop the rhythm.

Entire civilizations have collapsed while trying. You can't dam a river that wants to flow. It's like holding back the ocean tides with glue and rubber bands. Sooner or later, things will burst. And when they do, they'll get ugly.

You can't stop the rhythm.

When we try, people get sick. Chronic stress, digestive issues, inflammation, immune disorders, depression, addiction—all symptoms of a larger issue. And the more stagnant we become, the more medications we require.

Sooner or later, we all face disappointments. Illness, financial loss, death of loved ones, our own annihilation—these things cannot be avoided. They are inescapable. The key is to stop focusing on them and start living each moment with hallucinatory clarity. For until we learn to enjoy the ebbing and flowing of life, much of our time will be wasted trying to avoid its unpleasantries.

Much of people's thinking these days is at the mercy of "experts." We've become part of a colorless mass that no longer thinks its own thoughts, forms its own opinions, forges its own paths. Engaging in meaningful activity removes us from this monkey mind, and instead returns us to the rhythm of life—learning new skills, opening new pathways in the brain, keeping us deeply rooted in the flow of life. Our meaningful activities are like islands in a sea of chaos. They keep us grounded. They keep us flowing. They keep us dancing.

When engaged in meaningful activity, there is no death, no sorrow, no illness. Tuned into our bodies and the task at hand, free from the confines of our chaotic minds, we experience the present moment in all its glory. This is ecstasy—a drop of water returning to the ocean, our true place in the world, where everything makes sense. When we experience such moments of extreme clarity, we become one with the universe. We bring sanity to the world.

And this is important work indeed!

Life dances. It twists and twirls, boogies and hops. It bounces and wiggles, flickers and flops. It rocks and rolls, trips and tumbles. It jiggles and wobbles, rollicks and fumbles.

You can't stop the rhythm.

You may be asking why anyone should like to stop the rhythm. Let's just say mental illness is a tricky thing I cannot pretend to understand. Still, there are people in this world who would like to stop the rhythm. When these people are in power, their pleas and bribes and demands can be convincing. When threatened, entire populations can easily fall victim to the fearmongering we've come to know well through the media. This can make us frighteningly compliant. The key is to recognize this when it's happening. When we operate out of fear, we become irrational. We ignore facts. We disregard what's happening right before our very eyes.

"The only thing we have to fear is fear itself."
—Rev. Martin Luther King Jr.

Our beloved Earth—with its oceans and rivers, mountains and deserts, clouds and sunsets, birds and fish, plants and fungi, and industrialized human societies—is a dust mote spiraling in a snowstorm of 100 billion galaxies, each containing a trillion stars. We are stardust. Once we accept this inevitable truth, we can learn to enjoy the ride. Humans are frightened by chaos. We now understand two ways to deal with this fear:

> Latch onto a false sense of security.
> Find rhythm within the chaos.

Take a musical instrument such as the guitar: a worthless contraption of wood and steel, or a vessel for endless musical expression? It all depends on who picks it up. When we master our chosen skill sets, our meaningful activities become vessels we use to make sense of the universe. We can create great beauty in this world, finding rhythm within the chaos.

Staring at the sea, at the edge of the world, the last rays of light penetrating the western horizon, I reflect on our time in the Florida Keys. If Mother Ocean has taught me anything, it's to surf life like a wave that never ends, forever honing my skills, learning, mastering, evolving, until I can evolve no more. When my wave finally ends, I'll be ready for that comfortable chair. That chaise lounge. That front porch rocker. Like it or not, we all end up there. Or we die somewhere along the way. Regardless, I refuse to squander the best years of my life preparing for a comfortable chair I may or may not get the chance to sit in. To chase security is to chase death—missing out on life and all its great adventures.

What is ultimate security anyway? No more wanting, no more needing, no more pain, no more struggle?

Ultimate security is an empty promise because it exists only in our demise. Life is a sea of moments—you can't hold onto just one. We ride a good wave and wish to stay on it forever. But you can't set anchor on a wave. Waves come and go, yet the ocean lives on...

You can't stop the rhythm.

Enjoy this Book?
Write a Review!

_____

If you've enjoyed my book, the best compliment you can give is writing a review. As a self-published indie author, I don't have the advertising power of a major publishing firm. But you can make a big difference.

Honest reviews help other readers find me. It only takes five minutes, and the review can be as short as you like.

If you'd like to leave a review on Amazon.com, search for my title, click on _Customer reviews_, then click _Write a customer review_. Simple as that.

Thank you very much.

NATURE BOOK SERIES
(4 part series)

———

Explore the alpine peaks of the Rocky Mountains, the sandstone slot canyons of the Colorado Plateau, and the lush mangrove islands of the Florida Keys in Scott Stillman's Nature Book Series.

Have you read all the books in the series?

- **Wilderness, The Gateway to the Soul**
- **Nature's Silent Message**
- **I Don't Want To Grow Up**
- **Oceans of my Mind**

(books can be read in any order)

Sign up for my mailing list and you'll gain access to:

- FREE PREVIEW of each book in the series
- My ongoing blog posts
- Exclusive photographs
- Backpacking tips, gear checklists, and more

You can sign up for my mailing list at
www.scottstillmanblog.com

SAVE THE OCEANS!

SURFRIDER FOUNDATION

The Surfrider Foundation is dedicated to the protection and enjoyment of the world's oceans, waves, and beaches, for all people, through a powerful activist network. They fight for plastic reduction, beach access, ocean protection, and coastal preservation. Their power comes from people like you, from all over the planet, who want to protect our great seas.

If you'd like to get involved, please find them at **www.surfrider.org**

About the Author

Scott Stillman was born in Fairfield, Ohio, and then moved to Boulder, Colorado, in 2003. Wandering mountains, deserts, and oceans, he records his journeys with pen and notebook, writing primarily about our spiritual connection to nature.

Scott is the bestselling author of the *Nature Book Series,* including *Wilderness, The Gateway to the Soul, Nature's Silent Message, I Don't Want to Grow Up, Oceans of my Mind*, and *Wilderness Speaks.*

As our culture continues to remove itself from the natural world, Scott's books provide refreshing insight, showing that there's life outside the regimen—hope beyond the pavement.

He and his wife, Valerie, have lived in a truck camper and worked a slew of unconventional jobs to fund their travels and stay on the wilderness path.

You can find his blog and online home at:
scottstillmanblog.com
facebook.com/scottstillmanblog

If the mood strikes, send him an email at:
scottstillmanauthor@gmail.com

Symbiotic Relationships

———

I'd like to thank those who have allowed us the privilege of looking after their vacation homes. Your quiet and peaceful spaces have been invaluable for my writing career. We are always on the lookout for our next house sitting opportunity. If you or someone you know owns property in an inspiring location conducive to nature writing, and could benefit from the security of a physical presence while you're away, Valerie and I are clean, quiet, respectful, and will take great care of your sacred space.

Please email me at:
scottstillmanauthor@gmail.com

Thank you for the many ways you've supported me as a writer. I promise to repay you by writing a lot more books!

See ya on down the trail,
Scott

Made in the USA
Middletown, DE
31 January 2023